D1134973

JET TANKER CRASH

Urban Response to Military Disaster

JET TANKER CRASH

Urban Response to Military Disaster

Cornelius P. Cotter

THE UNIVERSITY PRESS OF KANSAS
Lawrence and London
1968

Library of Congress Card Catalog Number 68-16530.
Printed in U.S.A.

Preface

Financial support for this study was provided by Wichita State University, largely through the courtesy of Dr. Hugo Wall, director of the Urban Studies Center. The support and cooperation of City Manager Russell E. McClure helped me gain access to responsible officials in private agencies, public officeholders, and business firms concerned. Representative Garner E. Shriver and his administrative assistant Lester Rosen have been of inestimable help in this project and have shown continuing concern for the welfare of those affected by the crash. Frank H. Carpenter and Leonard H. Wesley, Jr., Wichita high school teachers participating in one of my seminars, and David F. Schuman, then a graduate student of political science, conducted interviews and participated in interviews with me. Thanks are due to these persons and to all those who submitted to interview, sometimes under trying personal conditions. Rose Isom, secretary to the political science department at W.S.U., managed to work manuscript typing into her arduous schedule.

I am especially indebted to Thoburn Taggart, Jr., chief reference librarian, and Russell E. Dybdahl, documents librarian, at W.S.U., not merely for their assistance, but for their unfailing courtesy and skillful aid during my four years at Wichita. The editorial staff of The University Press of Kansas have suggested editorial changes which contributed to the clarity and accuracy of the book.

All of the interviews were taped and transcribed. Tapes, transcriptions, notes, documentary materials, and a copy of the original manuscript are available for reference at the Disaster Research Center, Ohio State University, Columbus, Ohio 43201, which kindly indicated interest in the study and asked to add the raw data of the study to the Center's collection. Transcripts of interviews, from which the text draws liberally, have not been footnoted. Every effort has been made to avoid taking quotations out of context, although in the interest of brevity it has been necessary to be selective.

I have earlier dealt with governmental response to emergency in a book on the American experience, co-authored with J. Malcolm Smith, and in a series of law review articles on the problem in a British setting. Thus an inquiry in that broad generic framework is not anomolous to my past research interests and efforts. I would prefer, however, to consider the present study in the context of a continuing preoccupation on my part with the patterns of interrelationships of governmental units of all types and at all levels with each other and with intermeshing private eleemosynary and business institutions, toward the accomplishment of the goals which we have decided to pursue through group effort.

The experience of watching a KC-135 tanker desperately trying to maintain altitude as it banked westward after take-off, witnessing its sudden plunge into a heavily populated neighborhood with an instantaneous envelopment of what seemed to be a square block by a huge ball of flame, and then subsequent participation in the clean-up and evacuation, provided the main stimulus for this study.

CORNELIUS P. COTTER

University of Wisconsin – Milwaukee
August, 1967

Contents

Illustrations

Facing Page

Introduction

This is a policy-oriented, descriptive study of a disaster and community response to it, when an Air Force KC-135 tanker crashed in a crowded Negro residential section of Wichita, Kansas, on January 16, 1965. The attendant explosion took twenty-nine lives, seven of them the crew who could not escape. Had the plane not ejected considerable of its load of fuel before crashing, or had it made a gliding rather than an almost vertical descent, it is likely that the disaster would have been of much greater magnitude, destroying scores of additional lives and perhaps square blocks of houses.

Such an incident creates immediate and obvious problems and leaves behind it a wake of personal tragedy, dislocation, speculation, and community introspection. The response of public and private agencies, including the Air Force, was expeditious, organized, and efficient. It was not extemporized. Various persons with public and private responsibilities which would involve them in disaster work had been engaged for years in planning for the eventuality of a major plane crash in the city, which proclaims itself the Air Capital of the world and is adjacent to a major Air Force installation. These officials freely confess, however, that their planning (narrated in Chapter IV) was premised more upon the crash of a major commercial airliner rather than of a large military plane laden with fuel.

I have said that the crash left speculation in its wake. It is not the purpose of this study to inquire into the causes of the crash. As this is written, the United States District Court in Wichita has before it suits naming the government and Boeing Company as co-defendents. Yet opinions bearing on the cause of the crash persist. The October 3, 1965, *Wichita Eagle and Beacon,* for example, carried a story on the Air Force investigation of the incident under the captions, "KC-135 Pilot Attempted Correction. Mechanical Difficulty Crash Cause." And the comment of one businessman, quoted in the *Wichita Eagle,* January 18, 1965, that the tanker crew "certainly did a heroic thing in trying to miss hitting the homes in the area," suggests a then popular and lingering notion that whatever might have been the causes of the crash, the plane's vertical descent and its impact at an intersection adjacent to a small open field indicate the pilot had a modicum of control over a disabled craft and made a courageous and determinate decision to nose it into the field if possible.

Traumatic events leave legends behind, and the legends become a part of the factual picture of the events, regardless of their literal accuracy. The notion that the pilot placed the plane close to where he wanted it to go down—if it had to go down—probably falls in this category. Side by side with this notion persists the lingering and probably ineradicable suspicion that it was not by happenstance that the plane, in trouble, flew over and crashed into the Negro part of the city rather than a white neighborhood. A muted version of this theme emerged in discussions with Rev. Everett Reynolds of St. Mark Methodist Church.

> I think it is true that . . . one of the Air Force persons said to me, "Why, you don't think that plane really meant to do this, do you?" It was a guilt thing that someone had mentioned. It bothered him enough that he came and asked me and I said to him that I hope—I certainly hope—that we have no nuts flying for us. This is my answer because I hope that nobody is going to [do such a thing] deliberately. . . . This is my answer and I don't have the slightest thought in my mind that anybody would deliberately turn a plane to the ground to get themself a few people. . . . Though I do know that at the same time we must question why did he pick this area. . . . I think this is something that needs to be looked into in terms of this race issue, that there was the feeling, a very strong feeling this was the case. That if he had to go down, where is the best area to go down, and here is a field in a supposedly Negro neighborhood. If he must go down, this is the best place. It'll mean less. . . . We certainly tried to help offset this by saying that he was on flight pattern.

This "who knows, it might have been, but on the other hand it is impossible to conceive, yet we must not discount the far-fetched chance" attitude is, I think, accurately reflective of an undercurrent of uncertainty. "Why did it happen here, and to us?"

The *Wichita Beacon,* in an editorial of January 19, 1965, raised an as yet unanswered question relevant to that entire community and to other communities as well: "Inevitably there will arise the question of whether the plane should have been flying over a congested urban area when it was loaded with nearly 25,000 gallons of highly volatile jet fuel. Actually, of course, the Air Force sets up its flight patterns to try to avoid this. Even in emergencies, there are plans to be followed that should take a plane away from a congested area if the pilot is able to retain control of his craft."

In this editorial, in an *Eagle* editorial of the preceding day, and a subsequent March 2, 1965, *Beacon* editorial, and in anniversary feature stories retelling the events of January 16, the community's press echoed, reacted to, and reinforced a mood of introspection and a process of appraisal of the adequacy of community response to the crash. The appraisal, as with the Red Cross, was sometimes an indulgence in self-congratulation, and, as with the Disaster Committee, sometimes an effort to pinpoint inadequate performance and gaps in planning, and to attempt to improve procedures which had already shown their basic adequacy. A subject of enduring concern—concern which has intensified and found stronger expression as the disaster has receded into the past—is the adequacy of the procedures which the federal government has provided for redressing such wrongs as can be redressed and catering to the needs of those who have suffered. This is a topic which will be taken up in the final chapter.

"We cannot overlook the fact that this is a Negro community. The Air Force is white. The Red Cross is white, so to speak. I am using this term loosely." These, again, are the words of Everett Reynolds. If the Disaster Committee's plans were not premised upon a major military crash, it is equally true that none of the participating agencies were prepared to adapt their ministrations to the needs of Negroes of lower social-economic status. Subsequent to the crash, with some show of alacrity, the

Red Cross appointed the first Negro to sit on its board. Despite the occasional black face of officialdom (especially in the fire department and the Air Force), however, the crash was characterized by white response to a Negro disaster.

This situation affected the dexterity with which the relief efforts were carried out—those needing and seeking help ranged in their attitudes from submissiveness to suspicion and hostility. They were fearful of signing forms and did not understand the necessity for red tape; they thought the prodding questions of private agency and governmental representatives were evidence of hostility and impugned their honesty. They had been hurt; they were in need; the mass media had told them that money and material aid awaited them at the emergency headquarters on 21st Street, and they wanted it as a matter of right and without humiliating or antagonistic form-filling and interrogation. The agents for dispensing help sought with varying success to minimize the frightening mystery of all the bureaucratic procedures. If any agent expected gratitude for any aid dispensed to persons dislocated because the Air Force had planted a plane at the intersection of 20th and Piatt, however, he was to be disappointed.

The recurrent complaint was and remains that things would have been different had the plane crashed in a white neighborhood. The proposition is indubitably true, yet there is not evidence of discrimination in the administration of aid. But this is a point which has not, or perhaps cannot, be convincingly articulated to Negroes. Had the plane crashed two miles due east, surviving residents of the upper middle-class, white neighborhood probably would have abandoned their damaged houses, taken temporary residence in a hotel or motel, and called upon their insurance broker to get estimates for reconstruction and pay the costs of temporary residence away from home. They would not have been fearful of public officials, would have been quite positive of their rights, and would have firmly demanded immediate response to their requests. The suggestion of an expediting telephone call to their congressman would probably be a continuing refrain in conversations. Thus things might indeed have been different if the disaster had occurred in another area.

A final comment on the nature of this study: I have termed it descriptive. In their paper "The Methodological Challenge of Disaster Research," Ira H. Cisin and Walter B. Clark have written:

> Clearly, the opening wedge in disaster research must be a set of *descriptive* studies, detailing the behavior with which disaster research is concerned. Descriptive studies tend to be informal observational studies that attempt to answer the question: "Just exactly what happened?" Since, in any disaster, a great many things happened, it is perhaps inevitable that descriptive studies characteristically reflect the selective perception of the observer. The newspaper reporter sees one thing, the psychologist another, the sociologist still another. The descriptive studies serve the principal scientific purpose of introducing the researcher into an unfamiliar area and of steeping him in the phenomena to be studied more formally in the future. The principal purpose of descriptive studies is the generation of hypotheses, the encouragement of insights, and the beginnings of explanation.[1]

I have not essayed a contribution to theories of disaster or response to disaster. If this study is helpful to those engaged in development of such a body of theory, the aid is fortuitously, although gladly, provided. I have undertaken an inquiry into the relations which obtain between varying layers of government, varying agencies within the same jurisdiction, and between government and private institutions, in a specific context, namely, a disaster of somewhat limited dimensions. My framework for viewing and recording events is, perhaps, best to be gleaned by a reading of the introductory paragraphs of Chapter V, " 'Private' Agencies." I have also sought to record the perceptions of such private and public action upon the part of the immediately affected public, in this case a segregated minority group.

I

Operation Lucky Number

The KC-135A stratotanker is one of a family of jet behemoths —medium and heavy bombers, tankers, transports, and commercial airliners—engineered and produced by the Boeing Company. The original incentive to develop this family of aircraft is attributed to the August, 1941, decision by President Franklin D. Roosevelt and Prime Minister Winston Churchill to call for design studies for a bomber which could attack Germany from American bases. Thus in the event England went under, it would be possible to continue the war on the Continent from the United States. Although Boeing was a competitor for the design contract, it lost to Convair's B-36. However, with the subsequent introduction of jet propulsion, the Seattle-Wichita firm was granted permission to develop a turbojet bomber. This was the inception of the B-52-type plane, similar to but larger than Boeing's B-47 prototype bomber.[1]

In 1952, Boeing decided to sink 15 million dollars in the design of a jet tanker-transport, the KC-135. One month after the prototype KC-135 made its first flight in July, 1954, the Air Force had announced its intention to purchase.[2] In October, official production papers were signed and "just 21 months and 13 days later, on July 13, 1956, the first production airplane rolled from the factory." The Strategic Air Command received its first KC-135 on January 31, 1957.[3]

"Designed for high-speed, high-altitude refueling, the KC-135A is equipped with a telescoping winged flying boom. Aerial refueling equipment is all on the lower deck, leaving the upper deck clear for cargo or troop-carrying services. The deck can accommodate eighty passengers or twenty-five tons of cargo, or a combination of both." With a wing of 130 feet and a weight of more than 250,000 pounds, the plane has a range of 4000 miles, a speed of 600 miles an hour, and a ceiling higher than 35,000 feet. It normally carries a crew of four.[4]

The tanker crews "operate on an around-the-clock basis, flying missions in support of tactical operations wherever and whenever needed. Without the KC-135 and the ability of the tanker crews to 'change the range' or 'extend the punch' of the U.S. aircraft, the U.S. Air Force would not have the global air capability it enjoys today."[5]

By January 12, 1965, the 732nd and last of the tanker-transports was delivered.[6] The telescopic nature of technological and weapons-systems development is such that the KC-135 belonged to an obsolete weapons system before the last one came off the assembly line. Certainly the growing number of "write-ups" (pilot's report of possible defects noted in flight) on the older KC-135's would indicate, in the words of a maintenance technical sergeant, that by 1965 some of the tankers were "getting quite a bit of time on them."[7]

Since its introducion, the B-52 has been in the continuous process of modernization or, more appropriately, "modification," the industrial term for eliminating defects or adapting the plane for purposes other than the original. Following modification, the B-52's are flight-tested. These flights are conducted from the sprawling Boeing plant adjacent to McConnell Air Force Base in Wichita, Kansas. In 1964 and 1965 the 70th Bomb Wing, located at Clinton-Sherman Air Force Base in Oklahoma, provided "refueling support for experimental flight tests conducted by the Boeing Company under contract to the USAF."[8] The Air Force designation for this SAC-Boeing arrangement was "Operation Lucky Number."

We are concerned with the nineteenth experimental flight to be flown under Operation Lucky Number. The aircraft which made this sortie, KC-135 57-1442 ("Raggy 42"), and both its flight and ground crews had originally been assigned to the Pacific on a fighter refueling mission. By an irony of fate, however, a switch was made and the craft and its flight crew were detailed instead to Wichita and disaster: "1442 had had trouble with his boom and he was still in the air on Thursday and we were told that 040 would take the 'Flying Fish' mission [to the Pacific] instead of 1442 because of this boom trouble to make sure he didn't have trouble on this 'Flying Fish' mission. This being on Thursday, it was too late to get the orders recut for the other ground crew and get them paid on Friday so they could have some money for the trip." So the ground "crew for 1442 took 040 on 'Flying Fish' and the crew that was assigned to 040 took over 1442 while 040 was gone on the 'Flying Fish' mission."[9] Such shifts of ground crew assignments are not unusual. Staff Sergeant Curtiss Bristow testified that "I have been with other aircraft more than I have been with my own."[10]

Raggy 42 departed from Clinton-Sherman for Wichita on Tuesday, January 12, 1965, at 4:20 P.M. local time. It conducted a scheduled refueling in the Boothill Air Refueling Area and in accordance with instructions, landed at the Boeing ramp at McConnell at 9:50 P.M., having spent about five-and-a-half hours aloft. Captain Czeslaw (Chester) Szmuc, twenty-five-years-old, of North Royalton, Ohio, commanded Raggy 42. He and his six fellow crew members had left on what they thought would be a three-day jaunt—Operation Lucky Number missions were looked upon with favor in the 70th Bomb Wing. There are three types of such missions: "Red" missions involve launching from Wichita, flying to Clinton-Sherman, and possibly recovering in Wichita; "blue" sorties launch from Clinton-Sherman and could involve putting down at Boeing-Wichita; "yellow" sorties are for all practical purposes routing training flights, both launching and recovering at Clinton-Sherman. Captain Szmuc had earlier flown a "yellow" mission to Wichita, although it is not clear how many of his crew had been on similar missions.[11]

After he had landed, Szmuc reported to the Boeing representative, who would customarily meet Lucky Number commanders and "would give them the word on when they would be flying the next day and what their mission would be."[12] Boeing also arranged lodging for the crew at a local motel. This is an example of the difficulty in this day and age of distinguishing between governmental and private, between military and civil. Lt. Colonel John B. Taylor, Commanding Officer of the 70th Organizational Maintenance Squadron at Clinton-Sherman, testified: "Until some time since the accident, and I will say within the last three days, I was not aware of the fact that Boeing/Wichita was any different than McConnell Air Force Base. In fact, I always thought that this aircraft was going to an Air Force Base in support of some test mission. What the Mission was, I didn't know." Indeed he had not heard of the code name "Lucky Number." The question put to him was fashioned in the following words: "Let me ask it this way: You were familiar that your airplane went in to support this particular mission outlined under this SAC Operations Order you have in your hand, 83-65, 'Lucky Number.' I believe you have mentioned you were familiar that your airplanes were supporting this particular operation." "Yes, sir. I knew they were supporting an operation at that location but I frankly had never heard the terminology 'Lucky Number,' until this morning."[13]

On Wednesday, January 13, Boeing had nothing scheduled for Raggy 42. On Thursday, a Boeing representative called Clinton-Sherman to indicate that the mission had been scratched that day. Szmuc called to report that the general condition of the aircraft was satisfactory and that he was planning to fly the next day. The Friday flight was scratched. "Then," testified Captain Buswell, Tanker Scheduler for the 70th Bomb Wing, "on Friday Captain Szmuc called immediately after their second cancellation. I am not sure but I believe both of these cancellations were a result of weather. . . . At that time he advised me that Boeing wanted to fly on Saturday." Although the tankers deployed to Boeing normally adhered to a five-day flying week, Szmuc was willing to undertake the sortie. "Since he was already there," Buswell advised him to fly it and recover at Clinton-Sherman.[14]

On Saturday, Captain Szmuc and crew had already arrived at Boeing Operations before 7:30 A.M., when James M. Adams, Boeing test pilot who was then primarily concerned with Lucky Number flights, appeared.

> The schedule was set up for an eight o'clock release. The previous day the tanker crew had been

> briefed thoroughly by Operations, and I guess partially re-briefed because of the schedule slide. . . . The tanker crew—I believe it was the pilot, copilot, navigator and, if I am not mistaken, the boom operator—were in our Operations. . . . And they had already filled out the forms and had already obtained their weather through McConnell weather. They went to their plane I would guess at ten minutes to eight, maybe even before that. Although we had not been released, they elected to go to the airplane and stand by . . . to give them ample time for pre-flight checks, *et cetera*.[15]

There was initial trouble with the tanker's number one engine, but that did not disturb Adams. "I assumed if he's got trouble, we won't go; if he doesn't have trouble, we will go. He is certainly capable of isolating and treating his own problems properly."

There is testimony from numerous quarters concerning the appearance of the Raggy 42 crew that morning. The Deputy Commander for Operations, 70th Bomb Wing, rated it as "one of my better crews." Adams regarded the crew as "quite alert,"—"I wasn't . . . looking over their shoulders or anything, but they were progressing right along in an orderly fashion I thought." They sounded "normal" to the Boeing tower operator, and "real capable; real confident," to the Federal Aviation Agency controller in the Municipal Airport tower.[16]

The B-52, having ascertained that Raggy 42's engine problem had been corrected, "checked back with the tanker and told him we would be taxiing. They started taxiing about the same time we did and, in fact, I think I pulled out from our parking spot, which was on a westerly heading in the center of the ramp, as he was pulling out from his spot, which was heading east. He was turning south and we went south. Of course, we were going through our normal checks as we were taxiing and I assume he was too. We actually caught up with him as he stopped at the end of the runway on the west taxiway. We were parked behind maybe 150 feet."[17] Adams, preoccupied with his own responsibilities, was conscious of a light wind out of the northeast and what appeared to be a normal take-off roll by the tanker. He spent the next five minutes getting his own aircraft into take-off position.

At 9:14 A.M. Raggy 42 asked the McConnell tower for take-off instructions. Instructed to use Runway 36, the aircraft responded that it was taxiing. McConnell called Kansas City Center, which controls all aircraft movement in the general area, and asked for Air Traffic Control clearance. At 9:22 it asked Wichita Approach Control for release clearance. No aircraft conflict existed and a Federal Aviation Administration Air Traffic Control specialist on duty at Wichita's Municipal tower recorded the McConnell request and "released Raggy 42 with a left turn out."[18] Captain Szmuc at 9:18 advised McConnell he was "standing by clearance any time you receive it." At 9:26 the tower radioed "Raggy 42 . . . change to departure control frequency 307.9 cleared for take-off 36 left." The plane rolled.

Boeing Control Tower Operator Kenneth McKee was on duty at the time of take-off. He noticed "Nothing unusual. He used about 10,000 to 10,500 feet of runway. His nose gear came off the runway about 9,500. The main gear came off well after 10,000. And he leveled off at—I would estimate at about 1,000 feet, maintained that altitude until he executed his turn to the west or northwest—I couldn't tell which—and from all I could see it was a perfectly normal take-off for a KC-135." Nonetheless, McKee had forebodings. He picked up his glasses and trained them on the flight. "The reason I picked up the glasses was the fact that he had lifted off what I thought at the time was pretty low. However, he maintained that altitude clear on through and executed his turn to the west or northwest and started his climb. So then I laid the glasses down and thought no more about it, and they cleared our bomber into position and to hold and at about that instant I got a call from McConnell Tower that the tanker was returning to the field, that he had declared an emergency. So I called our Fire Department and told them the tanker was returning under emergency conditions."[19] The call from McConnell came on the direct telephone line between the two towers.

Delbert J. Massey, FAA Controller at the Municipal Tower, observed the flight on his radar scope, as he had observed many other KC-135 flights in the past.

> Everything was normal. I tracked him out and he went straight out on the runway heading. There was no deviation and the take-off roll was normal. I saw him off the end of the runway and about three or four miles north he called and asked—confirmed his release and I told him—I didn't have any reason to break the release that was originally given. Had traffic showed up, I might have restricted him or turned him, but there was no reason for it. About four and a half miles north he started a left turn which is normal to go to Hutchinson. At that time everything was normal.[20]

This was all in accordance with the course reported to the FAA tower by McConnell, and permission for the left turn was reiterated by the FAA tower well before the radar scope or communication with the plane indicated any trouble. "That is when the surprise came. After he started his turn, then he started 'May Day-ing.'" "He was well into his turn before his three 'May Days' came. He was well established in his turn."[21] It was difficult to comprehend that a loaded tanker was in serious difficulty over densely populated northern Wichita. Szmuc's distress signal "didn't sound too abnormal" to the FAA controller. "I just thought there was some small malfunction and he was going to come back. I knew he was in trouble by the 'Mayday' call, but it didn't dawn on me it was real serious or out of control. I cleared him back with the tower to land either at McConnell or I thought he might swing around and land at Municipal which the runway is capable of handling. . . . My first thought was to recover the airplane and get him back, but this never did come to pass."[22]

Mrs. Earl K. Duke, Jr. was driving east on 13th Street in Wichita, near the intersection of Oliver, Saturday morning at about 9:30. She observed a large aircraft departing McConnell in an apparently normal fashion. Then

> I observed the aircraft approaching my neighborhood (1207 Willow Lane . . .). This concerned me as my residence is not in the normal traffic pattern. Next I noticed it was going immediately over my residence. Next, I noticed the aircraft was lower in altitude than

normal for being so far north of the base, the aircraft was flat (not in a climbing altitude), and was flying at an angle. I heard a low loud roar (very loud), rather than a high whining. I stopped the car on 13th Street between Kevin and Willow. At this time the aircraft was immediately overhead. I turned to the left and viewed the aircraft above and slightly behind me. The aircraft was flying in a northwest direction, but the nose was more to the west than the northwest flight path of the aircraft. This brought my attention even more as I wondered why he didn't bank the aircraft rather than flying flat if he desired to turn. I then noticed a big white puff which was followed by a heavy trail of white smoke. These puffs and the trail of smoke came from the far right engine. I then drove my car around the corner to Willow and then continued to watch the aircraft. I now observed the aircraft was finally heading west, and was level and still low in altitude and not climbing. I was hoping the aircraft would return to the base as I felt he was having some kind of trouble. I then saw the left wing start to dip and the aircraft starting to bank to the left. I was relieved as I felt he was turning back to the base, however, the right wing continued to come up until I could see the top portion of the aircraft, wing tip to wing tip. Then the nose of the aircraft started down, then straight down, then disappeared from view behind trees. I had time to think its really down and then I saw a huge red ball of flame. The ball of flame was so large that I felt a whole block must have been wiped out.[23]

The evening paper, the *Wichita Beacon,* led off its Saturday crash story with a series of eye-witness accounts paralleling that which Mrs. Duke later provided to the Air Force:

An eye-witness of the KC-135 jet tanker crash, Thomas Klem, 1817 N. Edgemoor, gave this account of the crash:

"I had taken my son to Wichita Heights school for wrestling practice. I was returning home and driving south on Oliver when I noticed a phenomenon of a contrail. I couldn't understand why there would be a contrail at that altitude a little more than a mile from the take-off spot.

"Then I realized that it was a vapor trail coming from the fuselage. I had a good view and the engines appeared to be functioning normally. There may have ben some rupture of the fuel tanks."

Klem, who has 700 flying hours as a pilot and is a die-maker, said that the tanker pilot apparently realized that he was in trouble.

"He put the plane in a steep bank and appeared to be headed for Municipal for a possible emergency landing. Fuel appeared to be pouring out of the aft fuselage. There was no fire.

"Then the plane appeared to go straight down to the ground as it peeled to the left."

Another eye-witness, O. B. Hill, 1463 N. Charles, gave this account:

"I was driving east on 21st about Waco. It was a bright, clear morning and I saw the plane heading west on 21st and it seemed to be only about an altitude of 50 feet."

Hill, also a veteran pilot and manager of the Western Auto Store at 21st and Waco, added:

"The pilot appeared to be jettisoning fuel. He seemed to try to give the left motors a blast and get the plane up in the air. As he blasted the engines, the tail appeared to go straight up and the ship went into the ground."

Bob Kirkpatrick, athletic business manager at Wichita State University, saw the plane go down from his office.

"I turned to a man in my office and told him the plane was too low," he said. "I went over to the window and saw that it was real low. Then it banked steeply and went straight down. It wasn't completely turned over."

Gilbert Roman, Sedgwick county sheriff patrolman, said he was talking with County Atty. Keith Sanborn on the campus at Wichita State University about 9:30 A.M. when both heard a plane approach low with a loud roar.

"It was going west about 2600 north. It was in a bank at the time. I'd say it was flying at less than 100 feet and losing altitude all the time. At about 2500 and Grove, or so, something metallic dropped from the tail of the plane and a white vapor was coming from the tail.

"It seemed as though the engine cut off. Then it went into a steep bank and nosedived.

"Then there was a terrific boom and a huge ball of fire.

"Then I called the police dispatcher."

William S. Goodin, 1743 N. Poplar, was an eye witness to the crash.

"I was standing in front of the place I live. This plane was coming over low. That's why I noticed it. All of a sudden it looked like something snapped. A piece of the tail fell off. When it fell off, the plane rolled over on its side. Then it went into a nose dive and crashed. It didn't catch fire till it crashed.

"I've never seen anything like it in my life.

"When it hit it exploded. It even shook the windows over where I was standing." The crash site was about five to six blocks from where Goodin was standing.

"I caught a ride over there (the crash scene). There was a man running out of a house, crying 'Oh, my Lord, oh my Lord, both my boys burned up.' One of the man's sons was lying in front of the man's house burning. Just like a piece of wood burning. I couldn't stand it. I left."

One unidentified eyewitness gave this account:

"As I was going down 21st Street, I noticed a plane coming down awful low—near the treetops. I slowed up suddenly, drove into a parking lot and got out.

"It looked like a door on the plane was flapping, and something like water or fuel was spraying out of one of the jets. One of the engines looked like it wasn't going at all.

"Just as he cleared my head there was a burst like the pilot was trying to gain speed. Then there was big roaring sound like an explosion.

"The tail end went up and the nose straight down. The plane hit like a ball of fire."[24]

The tanker had "slammed . . . into a modest residental area in the 2100 block on North Piatt. Some 270,000 pounds of flaming jet fuel turned the area into an inferno. When smoke cleared, rescue workers removed the charred bodies of 23 area residents and seven crew members who died in the holocaust."[25]

Since it is not designated a combat-type aircraft, the KC-135, unlike the B-52, has no ejection mechanism. The investigating board surmised that "in conjunction with his MayDay call," Captain Szmuc "evidently instituted bailout procedures." But it was too late to get out, and the full crew, leaving four widows and nine fatherless children in Oklahoma, accompanied their cargo of fuel and merged their fates with the twenty-two sleeping people and one unborn child who were immolated.[26]

Colonel James E. Trask, base commander at McConnell, and Colonel Olin E. Gilbert, 835th Air Division commander, received news of the crash while in their cars. Instructions were immediately conveyed to the air force fire and crash equipment to go to the site of impact.[27] McKee in the control tower at Boeing saw a column of smoke start up "and I called 632 on our test circuit and said, '632, this is Boeing Tower. Do you see that column of smoke?' and they said yes, and I said, 'Well, check it out, I think it is our tanker.' And he says, 'Are you kidding?' I said no. He says okay. So he went over there and reported back that he estimated there was two city blocks on fire and it was the tanker and he requested all the equipment we could spare to support it. So I called the [Boeing] Fire Department and told them to send all of the equipment that they could spare up there, that there was an estimated two blocks of houses on fire and they needed all the help they could get."[28] Thus Air Force and Boeing equipment was dispatched to augment whatever municipal and county equipment might have reached the conflagration.

"One minute after the crash, every Strategic Air Command post in the United States knew it had happened. In Shreveport,

Louisiana, Lt. General David Wade, commander of the 2nd Air Force, was told the news, walked from his office to a jet aircraft, and was in Wichita one hour later. By pre-arranged plan, he would direct the Air Force investigation." Other officers with safety and investigative responsibilities sped to the scene.[29] The *Wichita Eagle,* on Monday, January 18, quoted General Wade as saying, "We don't know the cause" of the crash, "but we are going to find out."

An investigative board of eight officers was set up, testimony was taken in Oklahoma and Kansas, exhibits were received, debris was inspected, and the results of the investigation were leaked to the Wichita press.[30] Subsequently four mimeographed questions and answers were, in the Autumn of 1965, made available to the public. The answer to the first question revealed that General Wade's determination was not sufficient to achieve his stated purpose. It begins: "A specific cause of the KC-135 accident of January 16, 1965, at Wichita, Kansas, could not be determined due to the almost total destruction of the aircraft." Exhibit X, "Performance," of the Air Force investigative report, tersely concludes, "There is no known way in which the crew could have avoided this crash."

The paragraphs preceding this conclusive sentence, as well as seemingly contradictory testimony scattered throughout the report, will leave clouded the question whether others than the crew could have contributed to avoidance of the crash. This, however, is a matter for the courts and for lawyer-like advocacy. We are interested in the fact of the crash, in its human toll, and in community response to it.

II

The Fire Fighters

It takes five years' experience in the fire department, an intimate knowledge of the equipment, how it operates and what it carries, plus a good working knowledge of the city to qualify for the position of dispatcher. The dispatcher on duty will have an operator working with him, and reports to the chief dispatcher, a position to which he may reasonably aspire. The job of the dispatcher—who works in an old brick firehouse some blocks to the southeast of headquarters—is, of course, to receive all fire alarms and to dispatch to the fire the proper equipment and personnel from the proper company in the appropriate district of the city.

According to dispatcher Gene Reynolds, there are two basic types of fire alarm. "One we call a still alarm, which only requires one machine such as grass, trash, car, and such. Then we have a regular alarm, such as a house or building. A regular alarm is three pumpers, a ladder truck, and a district chief. That is what we mean by a 'regular assignment.'" Reynolds came on duty Saturday morning, January 16 at 6:30 A.M. to begin an eight hour shift. To his best recollection, he received a telephone call from a woman at about 9:30, reporting that a plane had crashed "somewhere around 21st and Grove."

Responding to the telephone call, Reynolds dispatched a regular assignment to the vicinity of 21st and Grove. The engine radioed back, reporting the plane had crashed at 20th and Piatt and turning in a second alarm. Reynolds tried to find out whether it was a military plane, "but I guess he couldn't get close enough to see." At this point the dispatcher used the direct lines to the homes of the chief and deputy chief to alert them and called the chief dispatcher to help deal with the switchboard, which looked "like a Christmas tree." There are seven ways to communicate to the dispatcher the existence of a fire, and all seven were being simultaneously employed. The crash was sufficiently remote from dispatch headquarters to enable firemen from that station to help man the telephones to call off-duty men back to work and to cope with inquiries coming from cities as far away as New York, Dallas, and Fort Worth. These incoming calls were from newsmen or persons concerned about relatives who might have been affected by the crash.

The municipal airport tower called on its direct line to announce the crash. By this time the dispatcher was already at work on it. To the best of Reynolds' knowledge, Boeing was notified of the crash by the police department, and McConnell Air Force Base and the County responded automatically and without notification. The police dispatcher also alerted ambulance services and hospitals. The fire dispatcher notified Civil Defense, the fire reserve, the utility companies, and the city water department. He tried to get through to McConnell, but discovered that the base fire department was accepting no calls.

In the lingo of fire-fighters, Code 1 means that there is no visible evidence of flame; Code 2 suggests there is such evidence; and Code 3 "means that it is a fire that they know they've got to really go to work on."

From the time he received the Code 3 from Station 10 (presumably closest to the fire), at 9:31 A.M., until he received the Code 4 signal from the chief's car 1 at 12:31 P.M., the dispatcher's job was principally to insure that reserve equipment and off-duty men were disposed around the city to cope with any additional fires which might be reported. As luck would have it, there were none.

Tom McGaughey and Bob Simpson had a golf match scheduled for Saturday morning. McGaughey is fire chief, and Simpson is deputy fire chief for Wichita. The sky was overcast and the day was cold. Indeed, at 8:30 A.M., McGaughey had made a phone call or two suggesting it was just too cold for golf and that he was going to spend the day working around the house, when he received a call from the fire alarm office that a plane had crashed.

"Well, a plane crash is not nearly as unusual as you might think because we've had a few of them down, small civilian planes. We've had them crash in the top of trees with no loss of life or buildings involved, and we've had them crash into buildings. Well, my first question was, 'Are there any buildings involved?' He didn't know. Was it a military craft or a civilian craft? He didn't know that." He was shortly to learn that this was no civilian plane crashing into a tree. "While I was still on the phone . . . I heard the first responding company come in and say that they had a block and a half of houses involved, and 'You'd better make it a double.' " This meant calling in a second alarm, to which two more pieces of equipment, a district chief, and all of the specialists in the department responded.

The Wichita Fire Department is made up of twenty-seven companies located in thirteen stations. The city is divided into three response districts, under the jurisdiction of a district chief. Fire fighters work a sixty-six hour week, alternating twenty-four hours on duty and twenty-four hours off. Taking into account vacation, sickness, injuries, and other factors, this would leave about one hundred men on duty each day.

Despite a long-established and elaborate system for communicating air disasters in or near Wichita, the first alarms were received from citizens, one giving the address as 21st and Grove, the second as 23rd and Jardine—the address of a residential school for the treatment of children with speech defects. "Then alarms started to come fast and furious. The operator later said they were all the way from 15th and Ash to 23rd and Jardine—that whole area."

Normal operating procedure calls for equipment on the way to an alarm to respond to that alarm, calling in if the operators see another fire on the way. In this instance the magnitude of the fire warranted the equipment turning from its directed route to the obvious site of the crash. By Wichita Fire Department calculation, the plane was airborne at 9:28 A.M. and it crashed at 9:31. By 9:31 the driver of the lead equipment had given a Code 3 alarm. At this point McGaughey "rolled." "I was on the phone and I heard his radio transmission over the telephone from the alarm office and said, 'Well, I'll roll.' I got to 21st and Oliver, and turned west. I could see that it was south of 21st, and it did extend over a large area, so I turned in the third alarm and the 'off duty shift call,' thus pulling back onto duty the firemen who had gone off at 8:00 A.M. that morning." This set in operation a pyramid type telephoning system whereby the alarm office notifies the district chief, who in turn calls his captains, who in turn contact the lieutenants, who call in their crews. In a little over an hour and twenty-five minutes, 136 fire-fighters were back on the job—principally covering the parts of the city left unprotected by the multiple alarm at 20th and Piatt Streets. McGaughey says, "You see our big problem is on a third alarm. In this particular case, we have nine pieces of equipment out of service for other areas, so we have to put other apparatus in service. We have two of the on-duty district chiefs tied up at one multiple alarm fire, as well as the chief, the deputy chief, and the assistant chief and all of our specialty people—this includes our fire prevention bureau, our vehicle mechanics, our electricians, our building maintenance people."

The task of a fire chief arriving at the point of disaster and taking command over men who have preceded him to the scene is problem-laden. Action has already been taken—action which implies a tactic, if not a strategy, for coping with the situation. The chief does not necessarily know the situation. He must appraise it rapidly, assert command, determine if wrong calculations and actions have been taken, whether, if wrong, it is better to ride with them or to attempt to alter them, and so forth. McGaughey comments, "Actually, as far as my taking command when I get there, they know the time I arrive through my radio broadcast. I give a radio code that I've arrived at 21st and Piatt, for example. On any multiple alarm, my ranking officers report to me at what I've classified as the command point. . . . They give me a quick resume of where their pumpers are hooked, the number of hose lines they have out and where they are, where they've assigned me. Well, I have to determine, if I think they're wrong, then whether I'm going to cancel out what they have done and bring in some more companies, or whether to live with a mistake if there has been a mistake made."

Jurisdictionally, when the city fire department responds to a county alarm, the chief personnel present place themselves under the command of the senior county personnel present. In this instance, the Sedgwick County fire department responded with equipment and men, as did McConnell and Boeing, and automatically placed themselves at Chief McGaughey's disposal. This is a bit of an overstatement. The conflagration, with a plane-load of burning fuel seeming to have set—indeed to be setting—the earth itself on fire, was so intense that at moments it was almost impossible to maintain communications between the command post at the north end of the fire and activities elsewhere.

The first equipment went in from the south end—Piatt and 19th—although the point of impact was to the north. The initial effort from the south was to curb the fire and fire potential by driving the burning fuel which flowed down Piatt from the plane back toward the point of impact and center of conflagration. The fuel could not—at least with the initial equipment on hand—be kept from burning, so that the effort from north and south had to be devoted to concentrating the area of burning. Thus the firemen sought to drive fuel from both compass points to the point of impact and concentrate the fuel consumption there. It was necessary to contain the burning fuel in order to make it possible to use hoses effectively to fight the structural fires. McGaughey explains:

> Our normal procedure on any fire is to come in from two directions to stop further extension—the prime thing in fire-fighting is rescue, then we want to cover the exposures and confine the fire to an area and then go into the extinguishing of it. . . .
>
> The first two hose lines that went into operation were washing, driving this burning fuel that was floating on the water back up the street so we could get our lines in to knock out the structural fire as well as the sheds that were out back of the buildings, the garages, the vehicles, trees, shrubs—we had a little bit of everything and some 200,000 square feet of fire involved.

Mobile county fire department rigs patrolled Minnesota, the street immediately west of Piatt, putting out grass, roof, and shrub fires. The Boeing foam truck proved effective in smothering the flames covering the fuel-saturated ground in an open lot to the northeast of the point of impact. The chief confesses to not having advised Boeing and McConnell, in preplanning for such a disaster, to report to the nearest city fire apparatus upon arrival at the scene. Before he could direct the McConnell foam equipment to the fuel fire, on which their agent could be used most effectively, the big crash truck had run over a piece of shrapnel and was immobile. A second McConnell truck and the Boeing tractor truck proved adequate, however, to extinguish the remaining fuel fire.

The Air Force seemed to wish to establish its own command post on the scene. This was natural, considering the number of Air Force people there. The chief continues that upon the arrival of General David Wade, "one of the military reported to me . . . that General Wade was there and he had been contacted by the Pentagon to come in here and take over—take control of this." This proved a minor contretemps as General Wade quickly explained his unwillingness to take over the direction of a fire-fighting force of 150 men, indeed, to do more than assist in securing the area. With police and firemen being run ragged, this kind of military assistance was more than welcome to the Wichita civil forces. Nor did they have any difficulty in recognizing the substantial and appropriate military interest in recovery not only of bodies, but of remaining segments of the plane.

Chief McGaughey reports on the strategic use of the city fire apparatus: "Now as far as the location of the city fire apparatus: We had one pumper hooked up at the intersection of 19th and Piatt, with three hose lines off of it going directly North. We had a pumper hooked up at, what would be classified as Ash and 21st Street. We had a hydrant line from Piatt and 21st Street. . . . We had another pumper hooked up at Minnesota and 21st, which was supplying our lines at the Northwest, and we had a pumper hooked up at 19th and Minneapolis, which was the other available hydrant." The crashing plane ruptured an eight-inch water main going up Piatt Street. This caused a pressure loss at 21st Street, to the north, but the fortunate location of a twenty-inch main at 19th and Piatt, which maintained pressure, provided necessary pressure and water to keep the Department functioning until the water department restored pressure on 21st Street.

The houses to the east on Piatt were of brick construction, those to the west were frame. The impact of the plane had sent vaporized fuel primarily in a southwesterly direction—the effect being that an entire block of frame houses between 19th and 20th on Piatt suddenly had their windows blown in and their interiors filled with burning fuel. "The first three houses south of 20th Street on Piatt were completely scattered all over the area. The floor area was completely cleaned of any partitions, any appliances—such as stoves, refrigerators, hot water tanks, even the bathing facilities, the bath tub, shower stalls and toilet stools, were completely blown clear out in the back yard. All the crawl spaces were very clean—about the only thing in there was some soil pipe that was left in those areas." McGaughey's men found chunks of mud on the roofs of houses a block away, and an Air Force officer guessed that its fuel content gave it the consistency and flammability of napalm. Deputy Chief Simpson, who was working from the south end, said: "I have never seen so much fire in so many places. It just licked every place up and down the street. There was no way of telling just how many houses were on fire. It appeared to me that the fire was in the houses, burning from the inside out, rather than so much fire on the outside of the houses. I guess this is because the fuel was sprayed into them, and, of course, the contents of the buildings had ignited."

High tension wires were down—a factor that some firemen forgot to take into account as they clambered over wire fences. This oversight caused some of them to take off "like Olympic hurdlers." Not only were power lines down, but a three-inch gas main ruptured at the same time the water main ruptured. These, the flaming houses, and the burning or potentially explosive fuel flooding the street caused considerable danger to the crowds of spectators who invaded the area. Spectators were kept at a distance by police who early arrived on the scene, and indeed, many of those within the fire lines were actively employed in handling hose and otherwise assisting the fire fighters. During one period in which the row of brick houses on the east side of Piatt threatened to go up in flame, scores of civilians joined in to help empty the buildings of their contents, which were rapidly handed over backyard fences for storage in houses on the next street to the east of Piatt.

According to McGaughey, communications proved a problem—one bearing correction. The county fire equipment and the sheriff's office operate on the same frequency. The Wichita police have two separate wave bands, with the fire department on still another. Neither the Boeing nor the McConnell equipment included walkie-talkies, which was the principal mode of communication between the command post and deployed equipment and forces, necessitating the use of runners to effect communication with them. The chief anticipates that in future disasters, the heads of cooperating units should be with the chief in charge so that they can agree upon directives. The concentration of the fire in a relatively small geographical area minimized what could otherwise have been a severely snarled communications pattern.

At 9:55 A.M. Code 4 was transmitted—the fire was under control. An area comprising five acres had been sprayed with flaming jet fuel, igniting and destroying houses, trees, grass, shrubs, cars, sheds, and humans. Twenty-nine persons—twenty-two civilians (eight of them under the age of twelve) and seven military—had been incinerated. Firemen and police, with air police from McConnell, were to remain on the job round-the-clock for days to come, the firemen withdrawing on Monday, January 18.

The number of persons hurt was relatively slight, and most were on the way to hospitals in private vehicles before ambulances could be summoned to the scene. The area was strewn with incinerated bodies, however—not a normal circumstance for a fireman. It is not the job of the fireman, given a whole body, to determine whether or not the individual has expired. Normally, such persons are removed from the burning building and dispatched by ambulance. In a disaster of this magnitude, regardless of state law requiring the coroner's permission to remove a body, it was necessary to tag and move the bodies and segments to a marshalling area. Tagging proved a problem, for the tags provided by Civil Defense were of cardboard which became difficult to read when stained from contact with body oils. The popping of crisp corpses as hose lines came into contact with them helped neither the morale of the fire fighters nor the condition of the remains. Although the crews were taken off round-the-clock site assignment Monday morning, firemen were on the scene through the following Thursday, probing for human remains, bits of wreckage, etc. There was some difficulty Saturday morning as the military at first gave permission for Wichita firemen to remove military as well as civilian bodies and then supermanded this, insisting that military bodies (generally identifiable by the parachute packs) be left as found.

Lawrence E. Black has been a captain in the Wichita Fire Department since 1964. He has a roving assignment, working as a replacement in four different stations in the city. He is a twenty-year veteran in the department and lives with his wife and father-in-law at 1501 N. Hydraulic. Getting off duty as usual at 8:00 A.M. on Saturday morning, Captain Black went home for breakfast.

> I was reading the morning paper when all of a sudden there was a loud explosion. At this time I thought it was one of the Air Force planes breaking the sound barrier. My wife got up, she came out from the bathroom and she asked me what was that and I said 'I don't know unless it was a plane and with this I looked out the picture window in the living room and saw a lot of people . . . looking north. At this time I went out on the front porch and I could see smoke rising . . . that could not be beyond 21st Street. So I run back into the house, picked up a jacket, got into the car and headed in that direction. At the time that I pulled up to the scene Engine 10 was just pulling up. We both pulled up in different directions at the corner of 19th and Piatt.

Engine 10 had come from 17th and Grove, one of the stations to which Captain Black rotated. Black recalls Captain Scott Herrmann, on Engine 10, looking at the 2000 block on Piatt, where all but two houses seemed to be on fire, and exclaiming, " 'Oh! What are we going to do?' And I says, 'Well, I don't know, but we have got to do it quick.' " It was at this time that Herrmann turned in the second alarm.

The men could not at this point tell where the plane had gone down nor where the heart of the conflagration was located. "We laid one two-and-a-half-inch line right at the south end of the fire because both he and I knew that the job was to cut it off—stop it from spreading. Not only were the houses on fire but the street was too." Captain Black responds to the question whether he knew at this point that a plane was down: "No. I had ideas that it was because on 19th before we got there, there was several pieces of the plane that had blown that far. So, regardless as to what it was, after spending as many years as I have in the fire department, it is just instinct that you go to the scene of an emergency and do what you can."

The first hose laid, Herrmann took his men and worked on the fire while Black recruited a crew of civilians to help lay another hose. There was pressure in the hydrants to the south of the fire, and Black proceeded to pull out some 550 feet of two-and-a-half-inch hose. "Realizing that this is considerable amount of weight, I had enough men on it to pick it up and run with it. After we got this into operation, I can say that I actually do believe that there was nothing that burnt at this fire that wasn't on fire at the time of the first emergency equipment reached the scene."

The first job of a fire company on the scene is to preserve and protect life. The men on Engine 10 quickly learned that the end house to the south had been evacuated. "The house next to it, in my estimation, didn't seem to be burning as seriously as the one south of it as this time, but right outside, it looked as if he might of fell just outside the door, lay a victim. This was the first victim I had seen. We did manage to get up to him but after examination we found that there was nothing we could do at this time, so he was covered." The only injured person seen by Captain Black was being taken care of by a neighbor. But "I was just sure that this time of morning, being a Saturday, that every house along there would have some fatalities in it."

Initial fire-fighting at the south end of the fire concentrated on the west side of the street, where frame houses were located, and, as earlier mentioned, was directed at containing the fire: "After we had pulled lines into operation, we knew that the houses that were further down were gone, there was very little that we could have done regardless, and if there were anyone possibly alive, it would have been a miracle." It was not merely that the houses on the east side of Piatt were of brick construction and did not seem in imminent danger, but to wet them down would have required crossing the street with hoses, and the street was on fire. One section of hose did burn in two, either from the street fire or a piece of hot metal, and had to be replaced.

It is appropriate here to mention that Captains Black and Herrmann, and later Deputy Chief Simpson, received vigorous civilian aid as they attempted to push the flames toward the north while simultaneously putting out fuel-ignited grass fires threatening houses on Minneapolis, the next street west. Later reports from a variety of sources indicate that there was minimal or no looting and that the spectators were well behaved, although they impeded access for equipment to some extent.

Chief McGaughey attributes civilian cooperation partially to the fact that two or more Negro fire captains (including Black) and numerous fire-fighters lived in the immediate vicinity of the concentration of Negro-occupied houses in which the plane crashed. Thus the fire-fighters were recognized in both their professional capacities and as neighbors, and the leadership problem was eased. Talking about the initial imperative to rely upon civilian help, Black says: "This is true. And I can say, not because of it being in my neighborhood, that I have never seen more cooperation. Every guy was just standing there, just waiting. I mean, all they had to be told was what we wanted done. There was many a civilian who got pretty wet from not knowing exactly how to handle hose and it getting away from him, but they never faltered, not one minute." There seems no reason to suggest that the behavior of people in the vicinity of 20th and Piatt in Wichita, Kansas, was innately different from that of any other people under similar circumstances. They all pitched in to help cope with a common problem.

Black was asked whether the neighborhood people placed confidence in him and accepted his leadership because he is a Negro. He responded negatively: "I don't know, I don't think they . . . of course, this could be true but I don't think that I once thought of it in this way. To me it is a job and I can truthfully say that regardless of where this might have been, it could have been any place in town, and I don't believe there are any white or black firemen on this job who would have worked harder than they did right here." Whatever post hoc rationalizations people might build into their interpretations of the motivation of civilians and fire fighters, police, and air police, Black seemed to believe that all had acted like people.

Captain Black goes on to talk of the process of pushing the hose toward the north, and of the shock of encountering new and poignant evidences of the human havoc of the crash.

> When you found time to turn around and assess the situation, what did you find?
>
> Well, I really don't know. I just . . . there were so many things that went on then that it was hard to say because we got the thing knocked—when I say knocked —got the fire down to where we were sure it was controlled. There was a house that had been burnt to the foundation, I would say, and I saw two small children that were burned, and I don't know, this type thing I don't ever get over regardless of how long I have been on a job, or how long I will stay. . . . But these two small kids looked like they might have been dolls that had burned. One of them looked like the head had exploded, the other like the stomach. I mean, this is the type thing that we looked at.

By Black's estimation, his group was about half-way to 20th Street when it met the men working from the north end of the fire, and everything seemed under control. Then came the further, distasteful task of methodically looking for victims:

> I had a crew and we were going around doing a lot of digging for victims and a lot of these homes were practically rendered to nothing but ashes. A lot of people would say, "How in hell would you know where to dig?" If you have been around this very long you don't have to hunt too long. It will tell you where it is at. In doing this, I couldn't say how many bodies we uncovered. I do know that there were four pulled out of one home there. Then we worked on the south end to the north

and it was the process of digging out parts of the crew of the plane. I never will forget, there was a colonel, he must have been a doctor or something, and we were—I had two men and they were—pulling stuff out of a hole the plane had made at the time of impact. This colonel said, "See that piece right out there? Pull that in. I want that." I said, "It is only rubber." That is what I thought. And we pulled it in and he says, "Yes, I want this. This is a stomach."

Deputy Chief Simpson was in charge of the logistics and tactics of fighting the fire from the south—ordering and disposing additional equipment and men. Robert L. Simpson came on the Wichita Fire Department in 1942. In the days when promotions were far and few, he took the test for promotion—some five years after entering the force—and made lieutenant. He has served in nearly every functional unit of the Department, gradually working his way up to captain, district chief, and then in 1962, deputy chief. He is a native Kansan, a farm boy, born and reared within fifteen miles of Wichita.

Captain Black, asked when his district chief and the deputy chief arrived on the scene, responded: "I had been there possibly one-and-a-half to two hours. He could have been there for some time and could have passed even real close to me and me not knowing that he is here because if he thought I was doing the job he could have walked right by me and not have said anything and I would have never known he was there. He will check the situation over and I am pretty sure upon arrival this is what he did and evidently what we were doing was in his liking or otherwise he would have given orders to the contrary." This is testimony not to disorganization but to the training of the various fire companies to articulate with each other and to respond automatically, subject to the checking or directing influence of leadership.

Actually, Deputy Chief Robert Simpson, by his estimate, arrived at the scene of the fire about eight minutes after the crash.

I was home having coffee with my wife. We were having a chat about what we were going to do that day and I had decided I was going to play some golf but it was a little bit cool and as I was talking to her, I heard my storm door rattle just a little bit. I got up and went to the door and looked up around the area to the southeast of my house [Chief Simpson lives in the northwest area of Wichita] and I saw this mushroom of smoke. Well, it was in direct line with Derby Oil Refinery and I made a remark to my wife—"There must be something over at the Refinery." I thought it was funny because I had never seen anything like that before. About that time my fire phone rang. The dispatcher said that they had a report of a plane crash in the vicinity of 21st and Grove Streets. I said, "Well that must be what I had been looking at," so I told him then what I had been observing over there and he said "Well, that's it."

In a couple of minutes I was on my way and lots of traffic began to develop in the vicinity of 21st and Market. Fact is, I could hardly get through. I was driving Car 91 with the red light and siren on. Even with the red light and siren I had difficulty getting through. When I got up to about the Stockyards Hotel I could see that it was south of 21st Street. From the time the crash occurred until I had arrived on the scene it was eight minutes.

When he got to Piatt and 21st he could see department equipment hooking up to hydrants off 21st Street to the east of Piatt.

I could see the flame as high as a hundred feet in the air. It would roll with the smoke and I could tell there was a terrific amount of fuel because I knew there would be something besides a small plane. I pulled in there on 21st and Piatt and started putting on my fire coat, helmet, and boots. That's when Fire Chief McGaughey came up. Chief McKee, district chief, met me and reported what he was doing. He and District Chief Sandmire were the two district chiefs out of nine in the department who were on the scene that day.

Chief McKee gave me all the information that was available to him at that time. He told me about what they had—I remember him saying, "We have one hell of a mess!" This is the first thing I remember him saying. And, it was established that it was a military aircraft. I asked him to tell me, "What have you done so far," and then I gave this information to Chief McGaughey.

The civilians present at the north end of the fire "weren't even moving, they were just like statues. I think the impact of this thing was so terrific on them that they were just kind of in a daze." His initial impression was that the death toll must be tremendous. Simpson was immediately assigned the south end of the fire and proceeded there with McKee, receiving news that two engine companies were responding to that area. He established where he wanted the hose lines. Like many of the firemen, he was a bit less than cautious in clambering over fences and received a slight shock from a charged fence. The utilities had been notified but had not yet arrived to cut service.

Like Black, Simpson speaks of recruiting civilians to help handle the hose. Looking to the rear yards on the west side of the street, he discovered that "everything had blown in that direction and you could hardly pass through these yards without tangling yourself up with a bunch of rubbish or something blown out there." He began to lose civilian help as they commenced to come across bodies. "This is where they said they had to get back. They had had enough, but I had some other people coming in anyway. I thanked them, but they didn't want any part of removing bodies. I don't mind telling you, it bothered me, with my years of experience."

Smoke, heat, and flame made it difficult for Simpson on the south to see what was going on to the north. "I just knew that they had lines over there and here. . . . I had the problem that the lines in front that were extinguishing the fuel in the street ended up driving this fuel and heat back up toward our area." Making this problem worse, the wind was blowing smoke, heat, and fire toward the southeast. The jet fuel had generated such intense heat that when hoses were played upon concrete, asphalt, or the remains of buildings, they created a vapor which, driven by the wind into the faces of the fire fighters on the south, was "pretty rough to take." Two firemen commented that "it almost tasted like they were drinking jet fuel." The men did have Scott air-packs which they could have used had circumstances become desperate enough—but these are customarily used only when men are going into a building.

Although it was difficult to *see* what was going on to the north, Simpson kept in touch with the chief via a walkie-talkie. "I reported to him when we—well, I suppose it must have been ten to fifteen minutes. The fire was under control at that point and we were discovering bodies and, of course, then he ordered me to the command post. That is when we set up the morgue operation. He told me to be sure that our people mark these bodies and not to let anyone else take charge of that operation. My training division were the ones that were assigned to the marking of bodies."

"Overhauling," the technical term for putting out minor scattered fires, cleaning up debris, collecting bodies, etc., commenced at about 9:50 A.M. by Simpson's recollection. The code four had then been given by Chief McGaughey. Simpson was called back to the command post where he replaced Chief McGaughey for about a half-hour while the chief probably conferred with military officials newly arrived on the scene. Returning to the south end of the fire after this duty, he first "began to see what the extent of the damage had been." Simpson had seen no hysteria—only a kind of mass state of shock—upon initial arrival at the north end of the fire, and he found neither hysteria nor misbehavior upon his return to the south. The spectators appeared transfixed by what they witnessed.

Simpson stayed on the scene well into the night, then went home to get heavier clothes and returned to the scene at about 10:30 P.M. He reports talking with one lady who claimed to have witnessed the moment of impact. He told her that if she had any information she should be certain to give her name to his people so they could contact her later. "She said she wanted to tell me one thing: 'I knew that airplane was going to crash before it did.' Of course this was just talk. I said, 'Well, how did you know that?' And she said, 'Well, it was coming right straight down,' and she said, 'I knew that big airplane couldn't possibly land on that little field.' . . . Another person, I believe it was a youngster, I don't recall—maybe ten to fifteen years of age; he was pretty excited and he was telling about the plane coming in."

Chief Simpson thinks that in a similar disaster in the future the procedures followed would be basically the same although they did discover some minor defects in the preplanning for disaster. Perhaps the most significant positive result of the handling of this disaster is that in future situations "our men would feel more confident. I think they actually wondered what they could do. I think that they feel now that they could handle anything."

However, asked if the department could have coped with the situation had the plane come in at a more gradual angle, rather than inverting, and had taken with it four or five blocks of houses, he conceded that under this circumstance there would be a shortage of equipment, and all available equipment would have to be called from any source whatsoever. In analyzing this response, however, it should be kept in mind that all firehouses were continuously manned with men and equipment during the 1965 disaster, and in the event of a crash of the type just alluded to, station houses might temporarily be stripped and civilians recruited, in addition to relying upon the county, McConnell, and Boeing for help. Emergency calls for equipment could be placed to surrounding communities to provide centralized service for any other fires occurring within the city during the handling of a disaster.

Chief McGaughey reports there were two critiques of the KC-135 operation. One was held Monday, January 18, and was composed of the fire services from Boeing, McConnell, Sedgwick County, Civilian Defense, and of course the Wichita Fire Department. "The main item was of the mutual aid departments not reporting their location and their arrival as they responded to the fire, in order that they might be placed by the chief in charge." McGaughey avers that he would have made the same mistake if he were responding to a county, Boeing, or McConnell fire, but the point was not to apportion fault but rather to prevent future error. The second major element in the critique was communications—or rather the lack of adequate communications—between the command post and all of the jurisdictions and elements at work on the disaster scene. It is interesting here to note that Dispatcher Reynolds on January 17 placed calls trying to find out how McConnell, Boeing, and the county were notified. Such was the confusion of the moment that this information was not clear. This may point not so much to the inadequacy of communications as to the fact that in a major disaster it may be reasonably expected that all responsible units will be or rapidly become aware of the situation. Communications may not be the key problem, initially, at least.

A serious problem was establishment and maintenance of a perimeter around the Piatt and 20th Streets area. There was not enough cord immediately at hand to rope off an area large enough to encompass the full distribution of wreckage, napalm-type mud splatterings, and, indeed, to keep spectators at a safe distance from broken gas mains and electrical wires. A further thought occurred to Chief McGaughey during this briefing. In a city disaster, there are trees and posts available to which ropes may be tied; what if the plane had gone down at Municipal Airport? In the future it would be necessary to have available rope and four-foot stakes with eyes which could readily be pounded into dirt or asphalt to define an adequate perimeter.

The second critique was held the Thursday following the crash with the ambulance companies, the Wichita Metropolitan Council of Hospitals, the Medical Society, the American Red Cross, and the Salvation Army. Although the ambulance companies had alerted the hospitals by direct lines on Saturday, no one had thought to take them off alert, and personnel and facilities were unnecessarily tied up awaiting victims who needed the attention of the coronor rather than doctors and nurses. The hospitals remained on alert until 3:00 or 4:00 P.M. expecting many more than the seventeen victims who were hospitalized. The problem of body identification tags also was discussed.

Another failure of preplanning noted at the second critique was absence of communication with the clergy. Since the Wichita Council of Churches does not include Catholics, Jews, or Unitarians, it could not communicate with all the clergy. A perhaps inadequate compromise was that McConnell should insure the presence of Protestant, Jewish, and Catholic chaplains in the event of future catastrophe.

III

The Police

With the consent of Chief E. M. Pond of the Wichita Police Department, the following two pages are drawn verbatim from his report on the crash.

> At 9:33 A.M. on January 16, 1965 the Police Department was notified that an airplane had crashed in the vicinity of 21st and Piatt in this city. The first report was that in all probability it was a military airplane and that it could be either a large KC-135 tanker or a large personnel transport carrying many passengers. So at the outset and until air force personnel arrived we were not sure as to the type of plane that had crashed. Needless to say, this created a tremendous blaze and immediately on commercial radio, the area became completely saturated with sight-seers. The first area corded off by the police department was from Hydraulic east to Grove and 21st Street south to 13th Street. Upon arrival at the disaster we set up a command post which was south of 21st Street on the west side of Piatt in a vacant lot. The crash scene was immediately north of 20th and Piatt. As additional police personnel, police reserves, highway patrol, sheriff's officers and other law enforcement agencies arrived, they were dispatched and assigned from the command post in the 21st block on Piatt. The Air Force immediately set up a command post in this area

also, as well as the fire department, the Red Cross, the Salvation Army, and other associate agencies.

As the Wichita Fire Department and the Air Force Fire Department fought the blaze, the police, with the assistance of those agencies mentioned above, we kept busy handling both vehicular and pedestrian traffic in the area. As the fire department began to get the blaze under control and law enforcement got the crowd in the area moving, the area was then drawn into a two block area from the disaster scene. The officers, assisted by Air Force Police, went through the area, moved all of the people not directly involved in either fire fighting or in the police function behind the ropes and barricades that had been put up to shut off the area.

A meeting was held by the commanders of the various units involved and with the county coroner, Wichita Sedgwick County health officers and it was decided to use the auditorium of the County Hospital as a morgue for those who perished in the disaster. Detectives were assigned with fire fighters and air force personnel in removing the victims from the burned residences. So there would be no mistake as to which house the bodies came from, we set up our own numbering system of the houses because numbers were obliterated and some houses burned to the ground. We put numbers on the bodies corresponding with the house numbers as they were assigned. Our police department laboratory technicians were assigned to assist the coroner in viewing and identifying the victims at the morgue.

As the day went on, the Air Force made arrangements for a vacant building one-half block from the disaster area. This was the command post for the Red Cross and the police department, as well as the Air Force. Because the military was involved in this disaster, strict security had to be maintained throughout the area to keep curiosity and souvenir seekers from picking up parts of the air plane. The impact broke utility lines, lights, water, gas in this area. The power company had electricity and lights installed in the area before night to assist us in our work. Officers were assigned to contact residents in the area to advise them that there would be no gas service or water service and also to make sure that there were no gas leaks in their homes; directing those who could be in need of food and housing to the command post of the Red Cross, Salvation Army, and Air Force would provide the same. If such an incident as this had to happen, we were very fortunate that the plane went in at almost a vertical angle rather than at a glide angle. Had this happened the devastation and loss of life would have been much greater.

As it was the actual area of devastation was confined to about a one and a half block area. Also, again, if such an incident had to happen we were fortunate in that this was a military aircraft because a great number of personnel and facilities needed were immediately made available. After the fire was extinguished, the air police were assigned to guard the immediate area relieving many of the law enforcement officers to work traffic in other areas of the city. It was the responsibility of the Air Force as well as the [city] police to guard this wreckage. Also the responsibility of seeing that the homes in the area were not looted, guards had to be maintained for this purpose for approximately ten days. For many days officers had to be assigned to the area to control traffic created by sight-seers. The police department, with other agencies in the area, had been holding a plan for this as well as for major fires, tornadoes, floods, and so forth. As a result of these meetings it is felt that the disaster was handled in as efficient a manner as possible. It should be noted at this point that the cooperation among the agencies involved could not have been better. The National Guard was called and responded immediately, as did the Army Reserves. Police officers from other areas outside the city of Wichita called to offer their aid and some arrived eager to assist in any way they could. I think that is a coverage of what happened.

Like Fire Chief McGaughey, Chief Pond was at home when notified of the crash. Upon arrival at the scene, he, McGaughey, and Colonel Trask, the Air Force officer on the scene, agreed upon the command post position to the north of the impact point. By 10:30 or 11:00 A.M., some one hundred air police had been summoned from McConnell to help cope with the situation. Pond, too, stresses the positive aid afforded by local residents. Although lucky enough to have some cars close enough to converge on the scene minutes after the crash, local residents participated in traffic control and lessened spectator congestion, easing the difficulties of apparatus in getting to the scene. The police have a pyramidal alarm system for calling in off-duty men, similar to that of the fire department, and within fifteen to thirty minutes the force on hand sufficed to relieve the need for civilian aid. The sheriff's officers and both the police and sheriff's reserves shortly appeared on the scene, also.

At that time on a Saturday morning, the police have as many as twenty-five men available on patrol. Fourteen appeared at the crash point shortly after 9:33 A.M. when their police dispatch headquarters on the campus of Wichita State University had received notification of the crash. Ultimately, with all of the forces mentioned above, and the afternoon call for National Guard help, hundreds of enforcement personnel were available to ring a wide perimeter around the crash site. Calling out the National Guard did not involve great procedural complexity, since the Guard commander was Captain Kirkpatrick of the police department, who was present at the site with Chief Pond. At the peak of the morning's work the police had about 140 civilian police and sheriff's officers and reserves at work. This number was tapered as quickly as possible in order to insure normal community service on that day and succeeding days. The air police helped immeasurably, for Chief Pond "dropped in" one civilian policeman for every three air police, thereby gaining a maximum perimeter with a minimal commitment of civil police. The perimeter rapidly contracted as bits and pieces of plane wreckage were collected and the security need diminished. Also, of course, the crowds lessened in density as the fire-fighting operation lost its drama.

Impact point of the KC-135. The crash spread flaming jet fuel over the field and adjacent houses, cars, and people.

Civilians help to man fire hoses after the crash.

Air Force investigatory officers arrive at the scene.

During the height of the crash excitement, a radio station made the false announcement that police would arrest any sightseers arriving on the scene. The police department, however, records no arrests in connection with its security operation at the fire. One motorist picked up a piece of wreckage as a souvenir; the license plate of his car was noted and the wreckage later recovered. There was some scavenging by youngsters, but the wreckage was returned by parents shortly. Chief Pond comments further upon the pacific behavior of the spectators:

> As I have stated, and know that the fire chief has, and others, we were certainly pleased with the citizen effort. . . . I was with the military when they decided that we should move the crowd back farther past where some of the aircraft parts were, so that we could protect it. I was in civilian clothes with my badge pinned on the outside, and there were some uniformed officers, and there were some military Air Force Police there, and we asked these people to move back. We moved them back nearly a full block. And not a complaint—this is almost unbelievable—usually there will be some rumbling and some, 'Well, I don't want anyone pushing me back,' but the response of these people that helped on the fire hoses [and] helped direct traffic before our officers got there played a great deal in the success of this whole thing.

Pond is also enthusiastic about the Disaster Committee and the extent to which it set the stage for coordinated and frictionless action by a variety of units: "I think that this plan, and the fact that we had talked it over, just made it go together. We didn't have anybody knocking heads about, 'You do your part,' or anything of the sort. And it was the people who were in charge of each group, we knew them and we were together. If we had an Air Force problem we knew to get hold of Colonel Trask. If we had a fire department problem, we got hold of Tom [McGaughey] or any one of the district chiefs that were there." This, he pointed up, was not to suggest that in a catastrophe of this magnitude, the first fifteen or twenty minutes are not going to seem utter chaos. It is thus all the more important that individuals and units know in advance how to communicate with others as well as to carry out their own individual responsibilities.

Chief Pond set up the command post initially to the south of the fire, and it was here that the ambulances initially responded.

> And the very first, when I first got there . . . they were all coming in there for assignments and I purposely set it there because I couldn't see anything north because of the flames and smoke. This was a large intersection; we had a patrol car there with a radio, and it was about the closest car to the scene, so I set it up personally right there.
>
> These things are fluid as could be and I didn't know what was north—I couldn't see up there until 10 or 15 minutes, until I circled around up north to see who was up there and what was up there. At about that time Chief McGaughey arrived and determined that should be the command post.

Within half-an-hour, the post was moved to the north, and the ambulances were asked to circle around to group at the new command post.

Like the fire chief, Chief Pond identifies the hospital de-alert as the main flaw in the handling of the disaster. He checked with the hospitals in the morning and found seventeen hospitalized, all but three at St. Francis. At 1:00 P.M. the number, to his best recollection, had risen to twenty-seven.

There were little or no jurisdictional problems between the fire and police chiefs, according to the testimony of each, during the fire-fighting operation. The police maintained access for fire equipment and controlled the crowds as necessary. They also helped with body identification and maintenance of the morgue. With the fire quelled, even though firemen remained on the job for some days, the job became one of security and clean-up. A round-the-clock police patrol of the scene was maintained until about January 23 so that every last scrap of evidence could be collected and insurance claims adjusters could be given ample opportunity to photograph, observe, and measure as necessary. This security watch was restricted to one square block, however, within a day of the crash. It was drawn from off-duty men so that the policing of the city would not be affected.

Extra duty involves extra-duty pay, and the crash made inroads of about $18,000 into the police overtime budget. Air Force reimbursement of an item such as this is a matter of conjecture, red tape, and above all, time.

Like the fire dispatcher, the police dispatchers were flooded with calls, many from quite distant places. Calls came in from all over the country; indeed, the London *Times* telephoned inquiring for information. The police also received telephone complaints from people who found that they had to detour around 21st Street on the way to the basketball game at the Wichita University Field House, perhaps a mile due east of Piatt on 21st and Oliver. An on-the-site complaint revealed that the command post had been located on the parking lot of a "private club"—then a Kansas euphemism for a privately owned night or "bottle" club. Chief Pond, to the admiration and amusement of his subordinates, referred the night-club owner to the Air Force claims officer.

Chief Pond described the shift of command jurisdictions in these words:

> In the early stages you have to have—necessarily it has to be in the hands of the fire department. And you have to satisfy their needs to protect the life and property involved. You are a cooperative part in law enforcement, where you help to keep the traffic away from them so that they can do their job properly. Then it becomes necessary for the identification of the bodies. It becomes a joint responsibility of the three agencies, the fire department, the police department, and the Coroner's office. And by having the plan worked out, this all worked smoothly and without any big problem. I don't see any reason for there to be any commander for this sort of thing. We are real fortunate in that way, in that we didn't have anybody show up and want to be the big wheel. We had a wheel there for about fifteen minutes, but he changed his mind after a little bit.

The governor and mayor arrived for a TV conference in the afternoon, but Chief Pond's reference to a "wheel" on the scene was not occasioned by their appearance. Pond confesses that at first he wondered about the utility of having these elective officials on the scene, but he shortly came to see that such a conference with leading officials could reassure the public that the situation was under control. In the course of the conference, the governor and mayor inquired about what had been done: "They were wondering if everything was being done that could be done. And so, step by step, these questions were asked, and each one of us as were involved in it related what we were doing. And, as I say, I realized it was an important part of letting the people know that all of these things were covered."

IV

Community Disaster Committee

Mention the Wichita Community Disaster Committee to anyone in the know in Wichita and the automatic response is "Charlie Straub." C. Edward Straub, manager of Municipal Airport (a unit of the Wichita Parks Department) is an old-timer in aviation, having learned to fly in the days when there were no rules and regulations—not even a license requirement. Born and reared in St. Louis, he watched the St. Louis Municipal Airport grow from a grass field to its present dimensions and moved from control tower operator and assistant manager there to airport manager in Wichita in 1941.

Much of his experience at St. Louis was in the control tower, which impressed him with the need for preparedness for emergency. "From my position of control tower operator, of course, I was intimately connected with accidents, crashes, and everything that had to do with that sort of business. I've seen my share of accidents, fires, and participated in them. Each time I was impressed with all the things that we lacked in communication, medical supplies, fire equipment."

The airport to which he came in 1941 was still under construction at the site of the present McConnell field, some miles east of the present Municipal Airport. "The runways were just being constructed, and the control tower I'd helped set up the previous year was just getting into fulltime operation. Our police department was myself and the other members of the airport crew. And our fire equipment was a chemical truck in which we had far to much confidence, I'm sure."

Straub recognized the need for cooperative efforts from his early days in Wichita, for he knew that a disaster at the airport would require the mobilization of quantities and types of equipment and personnel far beyond its budgetary capabilities. The old airport was located adjacent to the Army-Air Force installation, Boeing, and Cessna. The Municipal Airport personnel handled all fueling, while runways and parking facilities were used in common. Because of the physical proximity of these varied facilities the airport could utilize the equipment and personnel of all in the event of emergency. This impressed Straub: "The amount of equipment and personnel involved far exceeded our ability to pay for anything like this, so that we entered into a more or less cooperation and told these companies, 'Now you provide your fire equipment because we can't afford it.' Boeing got into furnishing their own fire equipment and the base got its own fire equipment. . . . We finally arrived at a full-fledged crash truck and our own trained crew, so we grew along with the others. . . . We came to understand on the field that it was a mutual agreement—no one had enough equipment anyway—if something would occur it would require everything that we could get together."

Crashes and fires have occurred at the airport and in the county, and some smaller aircraft have crashed within the city limits. Two incidents, especially, strengthened the inclination of the airport, the county, and the city to cooperate and impressed the city fire department with the need for more sophisticated equipment and methods to deal with the special problems of an air crash. One event was the collision of two B-29's northeast of the city. The second was a hangar fire at the airport, to which city equipment responded. Straub says, "The fire just leaped from one bursting airplane tank to another until it completely engulfed the whole hangar, so that instead of having a fire such as the men might encounter in a building, when gasoline begins to boil and spread and explode and spurt around, you have a situation that will put you back to where you just wait until it weakens before you can move in on it." The city firemen just did not have the equipment or the methods with which to cope with such a fire.

"When you throw water in on a flaming mass of gasoline, instead of diminishing the confusion, the water spreads the flaming material and accentuates the situation; so that confining the fire is something that depends upon equipment adapted for that purpose and the maneuvers and the operations of the various personnel themselves, have a great deal to do with how you can fight it and whether it gets away from you or not."

The federal government condemned the old Municipal Airport in 1951 and Straub and company moved to a new site west of the city. The new airport began operating in 1954.

> Now when we came over here from the old airport, we were thinking about the new problems we would encounter. Between '51 and '54, we had a number of meetings, talks about what our situation was going to be, because the equipment we were going to bring over here from the old airport was going to have to service airlines and fairly large aircraft, but we were not going to have the added protection that the equipment at Boeing and the military had afforded at the old site. . . . We were going to be farther out in the county. Actually the county facilities were closer to us than the city. Police protection and medical assistance were not as advantageous as at the old field, because Boeing had some medical forces within their own plant.

In 1954, a "more or less formal" pact was signed, under which the county fire department, the city fire department, the state highway patrol, the sheriff's office, Civil Defense, the city police, Boeing, and McConnell agreed to be on call in the event of a crash at the airport. Initially, it was assumed that telephone calls would be placed to those units as needed, but over the years a direct-line notification system from the airport tower was developed.

The Airport Disaster Committee met regularly between 1954 and 1964. It was composed of representatives of all of the participating agencies. In time the committee was enlarged to include private as well as public agencies including, for example, the Red Cross. Disasters were categorized into two types involving varying responses, and relationships were charted. The crash of a single engine aircraft calls for a limited emergency signal; a multi-engine aircraft crash might necessitate sending out a disaster signal. Since the airport had twenty to thirty emergencies (or emergency threats) a year, there was ample opportunity over the decade to review the adequacy of relationships, equipment, and procedures.

> One of these was an airline Constellation with 88 passengers on board. It called in over Emporia and said that it was losing control. The crew said they were losing control of the aircraft and they were going to proceed to Wichita—would we have equipment ready? Our disaster procedure went into effect for the first time. The response was magnificent, and this happened about 11:00 at night. The clouds were rolling in the skies, lightning was flashing, the wind was gusting. It was a rocky night and it looked like a storm would break any minute. Before that aircraft arrived we had 33 pieces of fire equipment out here and I know there were over 150 to 200 people, trained people, with their fire, crash equipment, ambulances, Red Cross—everything that the Civil Defense could do.

The plane landed safely and it turned out that air turbulence rather than any structural failure had been the source of the trouble.

Later, a Boeing 707 over Tulsa signaled that its crew had been advised a bomb was on board and they wanted to come into Wichita. By the time the airplane was in Wichita "we had a fabulous amount" of equipment on hand. "The emergency units were coming in by the droves, and, as I say again, orderly, very quietly, and very quickly they were reassembled in their particular groups and ready to go." Every emergency is a little different and affords an opportunity for learning.

Straub had assumed that the F.B.I. would take charge in a situation involving a bomb scare and that they in turn would be assisted by the local police. "I asked the F.B.I. man, 'Well, aren't we going to search this baggage here?' He said, 'Heck, no.

I haven't got time and personnel. I am just helping you.' How about the police in charge? The police said, 'No,' they were 'just helping' me. I discovered we had been playing this game all the time and I had the ball and didn't know it." Subsequent meetings outlined the responsibilities of airport and airline staffs in the event of a bomb scare. This proved helpful when a suicide actually exploded a bomb in the terminal building.

It may readily be seen how experiences of this type, coupled with a continuing and conscientious effort on the part of the participating groups could, over a period of years, build up personal acquaintanceship transcending jurisdictions and functions. At the very least, this rapport and common understanding of individual and mutual responsibilities would minimize friction and confusion in responding to disaster. At the very most, it could lead to a highly coordinated and effective response.

Critiques were held after such disaster responses. In these and in the periodic meetings of the committee, attempts were made to answer these questions: "Where did we fall down? How come this equipment didn't think it was notified quickly enough? How should we do it? How about radio equipment? Where will we assemble?" Finally, procedures were evolved establishing assembly points at the airport and personnel to guide various units to the point of emergency. ("On a dark foggy night, or if there is snow or anything like that, the airport can be a pretty big and confusing place.") Upon alert, the police close off Highway 54, which passes the airport, and the emergency equipment rolls in.

Wichita took the airport into the city limits in 1962. Straub had been taking Civil Defense courses. He was beginning to conclude that any community can be "shaken" by a disaster, but not "toppled," if procedures have been taken in advance to mobilize all private and public resources of the community, regardless of jurisdictional lines, for common and coordinated response. Beginning to think not only in terms of airport disaster but also of community disaster, he called the participating organizations in the Airport Disaster Committee together on December 3, 1964, and again—indicative of his sense of urgency on such matters—on December 24. As a result, a plan for a disaster alert was developed to cover any disaster occurring anywhere in the community. The minutes of this latter meeting are to be found among the appendices at the end of this book.

Straub was very particular about securing Tactical Air Command (TAC) representation from McConnell. He was, and remains, very conscious of the magnitude of federal emergency aid —equipment, supplies, and personnel—available at McConnell, and of the necessity to tie it more closely into the disaster alert system. Straub called the next committee meeting for January 11, 1965, the day the new Sedgwick County sheriff and coroner took office, because he thought new officials should be brought into the picture as early as possible.

> That was the reason we deliberately chose the 11th. As soon as we could get these new people into the procedure, because we held all our previous meetings so that all these people would know one another, who they were, what they did, so that when we met them at a disaster you were going to know who you were talking to and who was who. This was the important reason why we had the meeting called on the 11th. At the meeting of the 11th, as I recall, we had some 36 key people of all the emergency organizations in town. We now included the ambulances, the hospital staffs, medical associations, the medical council, national defense transportation, and all these other units that we previously had not focused into this procedure quite intimately. We discussed the procedures, told each other what they were supposed to do, by whom they were to be alerted, to see whether they approved of it, changes were made, and then we discussed an actual establishment of a simulated disaster. Of course I had at that time in mind establishing this on the Municipal Airport where we could more or less control it.
>
> We discussed what the coroner was going to do, what the police were going to do, what the Air Force was going to do, the county fire department, the city fire department, the postal authorities, the Federal Aviation. We went through where the morgue was going to be, the command post and all this and that. Who had what.

> We even discussed marking bodies, marking locations. We went through everything that we could think of and simulate. We went through and discussed and this was all put on a format that we could more or less follow and each took a copy of it home to make corrections that he could.

On January 15, Kenneth Thompson, operator of the Gold Cross Ambulance Service, met with Straub in the latter's office to report on a task he had been assigned at the meeting of the 11th. The medical people present had pointed out that it would be a mistake to count on using semi-trailers provided by the national defense transportation group, for hauling bodies or patients. The doctors thought such treatment would kill more people than it would help. Vehicles carrying from two to four people had to be found. Thompson had canvassed the funeral parlors in town and been assured the use of seventeen mortuary vehicles, in addition to ten ambulances operated by the Gold Cross and Metropolitan services. Meanwhile, the post office had assured Straub that five of its vehicles could be used for emergency ambulance service. "On the night of the 15th, Mr. Thompson went home with thirty-two usable vehicles for the call that he was going to get in the morning." Although the simulated emergency was scheduled for March, the call, of course, came the next morning, Saturday, January 16, 1965.

Charles Straub was in the park department office in town when he received word by telephone of the disaster. He did not go to the scene but returned immediately to the airport.

> I would have been a spectator, and they had enough of those, I'm sure. And my first duty then was to be assured that this place [Municipal Airport] stayed intact. Our participation in the January 16th disaster was very limited. Actually we didn't move from the airport here. The equipment that we had here at the time consisted of a piece of regular fire equipment which belongs to the Wichita Fire Department, and that crew stayed on the field. My first call on being advised of this disaster was to check our own airport situation to see that whether or not this group was going to leave the

field we would be able to do whatever we could do . . . so that if we had a crash or disaster at the airport we could cope with it.

The Municipal tower (which, incidentally, is under FAA rather than airport jurisdiction) warned aircraft away from the crash site but did little more. Scheduled flights and Municipal itself appear to have been unaffected by the disaster.

Ironically, in that the community disaster plan had originated as an airport disaster plan, the airport played little role in the response to the KC-135 crash. A number of people, including the Red Cross director, assumed that the initial word of the crash had come from the Municipal tower—traditionally thought of as the nerve center of communications—since the assumption always had been, until December, 1965, that the disaster would occur at the airport. However, the Municipal tower did not give the alert, and *if* (one must underscore it because of the varying accounts received from varying sources) the KC-135 was given McConnell clearance to land at either Municipal or McConnell, Straub had no word of this.

> Our control tower was not in contact with the military aircraft and if that was done it was just a line broadcast by the control tower at the McConnell Air Force Base which meant that they were ready to receive him or he's cleared to land here, I suppose. If they mentioned this, this would probably have been relayed from one tower to the other or to their APC center over here, but I'm not aware whether this took place.
>
> Actually, there is no way you can limit a pilot as to where he's going to go when he has an emergency. We have had aircraft land here on emergency when he said he was on fire and he's carrying five-inch bazooka detonators. This has brought us up in our chairs, to be sure, but if an aircraft does this there isn't much you can insist upon a pilot in a burning airplane with five-inch live detonators do by way of alternative. He's thinking about a number of things and he's more apt to come in and land the airplane and stop it wherever he can and dive out. We have tried to select places for him to do

> this if he will, but we have no real assurance of just where he is, although we certainly don't want him pulling blindly up in front of our terminal building and then say he's on fire and he's got these five-inch detonators on board.

The Community Disaster Committee gathered on January 27 to review the January 16 operations, to identify errors in preplanning, and to improve planning and preparation for any future disaster. (Reports on this meeting and two others held on February 18 and April 5 are presented at length in the appendices.) Charles Straub found, much to his surprise, that attention had never been given to ending a disaster alert. "I found much to my surprise that I had never figured on stopping an emergency alert because here at the airport we have a perfect control. Whenever the emergency was over, we advised the parties and everybody left. But, we had forgotten how quickly we had changed from an airport disaster plan to a community disaster plan. In throwing these hospitals and the other agencies into the alert, we had a vast army of people standing by who didn't know just where they were in the conduct of the emergency so as to release these doctors and nurses and the requisition of cots and medical supplies. We had to incorporate these changes to follow up, to advise these people when the emergency was over."

It has already been mentioned that the disaster committee had not included any clergy in its plan. This has been resolved satisfactorily to Straub by McConnell's agreement to supply chaplains of the three major faiths.

V

Private Agencies

Working in addition to and in conjunction with the government, business, private eleemosynary, and other private or quasi-private institutions perform many social functions commonly thought of in our society as "government" activities. This is true in times of "normalcy" as well as in times of emergency. It is a simple fact which goes counter to the popular image that there exist two distinct and separate realms of activity in American society, one public and one private. Certain functions, so the over-simplification goes, are inherently public in nature and should be performed by governmental bodies. Certain are private in nature and should be left to private profit-making or philanthropic endeavor.

The fact of the matter is that public and private performance of social functions are so intermixed today that one can apply to this sphere of social experience the analogy which Morton Grodzins has applied to federalism in an effort to abolish the notion of three discrete or compartmented tiers of government in the United States: national, state, and local. "The federal system is not accurately symbolized by a neat layer cake of three distinct and separate planes. A far more realistic symbol is that of the marble cake. Wherever you slice through it you reveal an inseparable mixture of differently colored ingredients. There is no neat horizontal stratification. Vertical and diagonal lines almost obliterate the horizontal ones, and in some places there are unexpected whirls and an imperceptible merging of colors, so that it is difficult to tell where one ends and the other begins."[1]

Southwestern Bell Telephone Company

Southwestern Bell's parent company, A.T. and T., is a prime example of this point. American Telephone and Telegraph and its employees operate in many capacities under an infinite number of governmental jurisdictions and perform functions which are difficult to classify as clearly public or private in nature. It has a partnership with the defense department, having engineered and managed construction of the Distant Early Warning Line across the Arctic North. Its engineers "designed, and have helped to build, maintain, and operate communications for the Ballistic Missile Early Warning System and the SAGE system of air defense. They are now taking a major part in the development and construction of a new military communication system called Autovon for short, that will have capabilities of a new order."[2] As a stockholder in the Communications Satellite Corporation, a hybrid institution co-managed by appointed directors from the government and from private communications industry, A.T. and T.'s status as a private institution becomes more and more questionable.

As with all business establishments, especially in the communications and utilities fields, the telephone company has public responsibilities to discharge locally in time of disaster. There is a point at which the normal routine of business life gives way to the exigencies of untoward occurrences, and the profit-motive becomes irrelevant to the service performed. Thus it was with Southwestern Bell's Southern Kansas Division, headquartered in Wichita, on January 16, 1965.

John Oxler, division head, returned from a shopping trip with his wife and children when he heard of the crash on the radio. He immediately received a telephone call from the sales and service manager Louis Latimer reporting that Bell servicemen were in the crash area, that damage to telephone equipment was not extensive, and that mobile cars at the scene were providing satisfactory service. The Air Force wanted adequate circuits to handle a major investigation. Oxler called Gene Shnell, a neighbor and the head of plant department, arranging to pick him up on the way to the affected area. Being in a company car, they were allowed to park close to the scene of the crash. A brief inspection revealed that "what had been damaged

Firemen inspect the smoldering foundation of a demolished house.

Some victims were trapped by burning jet fuel in cars, others in houses.

Military personnel inspect the crater created by the plane's impact.

Wrecked engines of the KC-135 are returned to McConnell Air Force Base for investigation.

as far as the actual telephone equipment in the area . . . was just the small cables serving between two rows of houses. I believe there were two of them damaged and this isn't major. It didn't require finding cable that we don't have in the community or take a long time to repair.

"We then went to where the mobile cars were to see that everything was in order there, and found that the cars were working satisfactorily. They were, as I remember, close to running out of gas. We went in and talked with the military people about what they thought their demands would be in the area."

The telephone men learned that the Air Force was in process of picking a headquarters site and wanted some telephones connected directly from the site, when selected, to the McConnell switchboard.

The telephone company's problems were not confined to providing emergency service at the site. "The other problem we had . . . that I think bothered us later on, was the effect the announcement had in other parts of the country. Everybody knew somebody in Wichita and started calling in here. It jammed our equipment; we couldn't get all those calls through." The personnel problem which thus resulted resolved itself largely through the initiative of individual Bell employees who, hearing of the crash, streamed back to their jobs.

> The thing kind of worked itself out partly; some of them came in of their own accord. This is pretty common in the telephone business. It's just like the men that came in when they knew they had the crash out there. Some of them came in of their own accord and some were called out. The supervisory people over in that part of the business came down to organize it. I received calls from our people in Topeka and in St. Louis telling me that the problem was showing up in various places in the country and suggesting things we might do to help the situation. You'll recall, it was in northeast Wichita. Well, of course, this is one-fourth of the city and some people might know somebody in that quarter, or might not know where somebody lives in Wichita. Also there was one TV announcement where in

the confusion the announcer mentioned that it was in northwest Wichita, so this probably added more to the problem. But this eventually settled itself down and I guess as soon as people found out that it didn't injure somebody they knew, or did, and as soon as better information was given out over the news media.

The thing that we saw, from a telephone standpoint that would be the most difficult, was that they wanted some stations, some telephones connected directly to the McConnell switchboard. While this under normal circumstances is not difficult when you have some time, McConnell is in the southeast part of our MUrray central office so we'd have the line running from there to the office near Douglas and Oliver, running down to Second and Topeka (the downtown switching office) and then out to the crash site, about Twenty-first and Piatt. This particular area where the plane hit was right at the edge of this downtown serving area—right at the borderline—so it was quite a reach and when you extend the service this far, you have the problem of whether you can still hear on it (we call it transmission). There was going to have to be some engineering work done at the offices, to get this to work. We saw a coordination problem between the air base and the men in each of these offices and then out at the site.

We got direct lines in. I forget the timing now, but it was in the evening when we had the stations off the switchboard in. Before that we had put in several straight lines (just regular telephones). We had put them in for the Air Force, for the Red Cross, and for another group. The headquarters was set up then at the grocery store.

The Air Force, to really be well organized, set up a pretty good arrangement within that building—where people could come and talk with the Air Force people, these people who were injured through the damaged homes or had family injuries. It also provided the Red Cross a place from which to operate. They also set up kind of a headquarters office where I remember that Dr.

> Bauman, the governor, the mayor, the head of the National Guard, the coroner, and I sat in on a meeting. A couple of others sat and this was in the late afternoon after the governor had flown in and he just kind of verified that everything was being done and that everybody had what they needed to do the necessary things, and it was kind of a staff meeting really.
>
> The most use made of the telephones in the cars was by the Air Force in passing information around to the Air Force units in the country on what had happened and what was needed in getting the people in to take care of the immediate emergency and the investigation afterward. They talked to people from the Defense Department in Washington and from the Air Force office and the like.

Response to emergency is a routine part of the training of telephone employees:

> Each man with his job is informed of what his responsibilities are in an emergency. Each of the departments, the traffic people are informed, or operators for instance, that when these emergencies arise extra operators will be needed. Our repair people are usually the first in demand in this type of thing and construction people are on call not only for local disasters but for disasters elsewhere. We even sent them down to the hurricane area. We had a trainload that picked up a load of repair crews in Topeka and repair crews in Wichita and a system established whereby men took their own tools and trucks with them. A construction crew is not much good without equipment. We have a general disaster plan. These things all take on a different view. I was in Rusken Heights after the tornado. A good many of our people were involved when Udall (a small Kansas community near Wichita which was wiped out by a tornado in 1956) was hit. Just the other night we had repair crews in Cassoday which isn't in the territory we serve, but we do bring the lines into

> it, and I got a call that night from the district manager that the circuits to Cassoday were out but that they would be in within a couple of hours. The service into there wasn't a major problem but there were some serious problems in town with telephone services and that we had two mobile cars in the area so that people could call out, and he gave me the name of the man and the number of one of the cars in case I had to get in touch with them. We have a group who handles the contacting of the people involved. In this case, of course, it was the Air Force and their needs are complex and different than it would be if it had just been those residences involved. They needed some special services up there and as I say this was a rather difficult place because it was on the edge of a wiring area. Not real difficult in that you couldn't do it, but it took some working out in two different offices, and this took some time.

Sometimes a utility will draw up a retrospective cost analysis and attempt to recoup part of the loss incurred in responding to or as a result of a disaster. Oxler recalled that Southwestern Bell had "tried to put some figures together" on the Kansas City flood.

> We didn't do it in this case. Our losses were pretty nominal really. We lost one fifty pair cable and the telephone equipment in some of those houses and leading into those houses. We did have some time of course in the people who were out there but we never, in this case, because it wasn't of tremendous size, not really going to affect the overall operation of the company as such. We didn't put together any total or any figures. And of course, a lot of this time really doesn't cost you. The supervisory time and that, of course, this is a part of their job. This goes on anyway. There was quite a bit of overtime involved in this but not really major for a city this size. Ours wasn't the biggest problem out there. In fact, putting in the telephone service for the Air Force was the biggest part of our job.

Kansas Gas and Electric Company

There can be no doubt that prior planning and organization greatly affected community response to the crash of the KC-135 in Wichita. Nor should one underestimate the importance placed upon communications in the planning for a disaster in Wichita. Yet two facts stand out in connection with the crash, one a matter of happenstance, the other an important facet of community structure and process. The first is that an amazing number of individuals with formal responsibilities for coping with the disaster learned of the crash in the most direct and personal manner possible: their senses apprised them of it. As in many other cases, thus it was with Robert Matson, division line supervisor for Kansas Gas and Electric Company, who "happened to be out in the area and heard the explosion and saw the big plume of smoke and fire shoot up in the air." He immediately reported in to the K.G. and E. service operator and informed him there had been an explosion in the north part of Wichita. The second fact is that in any large community there exist multiple formal communications systems, sometimes interconnected, sometimes not, which will independently apprise public and private agencies of a departure from normalcy in any function which concerns them. This information may be disseminated simultaneously and automatically or it may become common property only after some delay.

Both of these factors affected the carefully laid plan for the Municipal Airport tower to serve as the communications hub in the event of an air disaster and accounted for its inefficiency on this occasion. Had the crash occurred at the airport, the FAA tower would have been the communications center. The disaster scheme, which had begun as an airport disaster scheme and had spread to community dimension, however, failed to take into account the multitudinous communications systems which, in an extemporaneous situation such as this, made it unnecessary to have a centralized point to spread word of the disaster; the underlying framework of these systems, built by meticulous and frequent practice, led to an unanticipated source of communication.

A utility company providing electric power to a community the size of Wichita is likely to have a number of substations, each with the responsibility of insuring continuous service to a particular section (perhaps a quadrant) of the city. As a residence has fuses and circuit breakers, a substation has circuit breakers and alarms which provide split-second information on the use of electricity, overloads, and irregularities within the system.

On Saturday morning at 9:31 a supervisory control alarm was received in the K.G. and E. service operator's office at Piatt and Central. This showed that a circuit had tripped in the substation at 17th and Emporia, which in turn indicated trouble in the vicinity of 20th and Piatt. At 9:32 the service operator dispatched a radio trouble vehicle, manned and on duty at all times, to ascertain the cause and magnitude of the trouble. Thus, as the fire and police departments picked up their information through empirical observation and sophisticated communications, and as the Boeing and McConnell towers followed the craft down, K.G. and E. recorded the moment of impact at 9:31, independently of other communications systems.

Also independently, and with uncalculated coordination, it took responsive action. By 9:40, commercial broadcasting stations were reporting an air crash, adding to the information available at the Piatt and Central office, and by 9:45 the emergency crew had isolated the immediate area of the disaster and restored electrical power to peripheral areas.

Electrical circuits or "section switches," located on poles, control the flow of electricity to relatively large areas—numbers of square blocks. At practically every street or alley, an additional "lateral" switch controls a single block of houses. In case of trouble on a block—such as a fire—the lateral switch can be cut off until the immediately affected area is safe, after which power is restored. In this case, the section switch and lateral switches proximate to it "just simply ran down into the crash area and disappeared in the fire." The two-man emergency crew used bolt cutters to sever electric cable and isolate the impact area from other section switches; lateral switches in the neighborhood were then connected with working section switches and power was restored. This was automatic assessment of and response to a situation on the part of highly trained technicians, who must operate at their own discretion as they see fit under the circumstances.

An electric utility company lives with disaster of all magnitudes. Its executives may have dual roles to play, depending upon the circumstances. A national military emergency, for example, can send them scurrying for assigned duty posts and to the performance of public roles; but most emergencies call for "routine" response to fire, flood, tornado, air or other disaster. In this case, the initial K.G. and E. response was seemingly routine and automatic—a response that was taken for granted by other agencies with governmental or private responsibilities in connection with the disaster, and by the public directly affected.

Service having been restored to all inhabited houses within about an hour-and-a-quarter after the crash, Division Manager George Weckel and Division Line Supervisor Robert Matson conferred on the next steps to be taken. The Air Force, police, and fire departments would have individual and cooperative needs, some of which must be ascertained and some of which could be anticipated. The area was surveyed to determine these. Temporary circuits were run in to provide electrical service to the command post area. Next, electricity had to be switched on at the Air Force headquarters, which had been located in an empty store in a shopping center on 21st Street, practically adjacent to the disaster area.

Then came the problem of area illumination. The street lights had been destroyed, yet even more illumination than was normally provided by street lights would be needed by Air Force, fire department, and police department crews working through the night. About five extra poles were erected "and lights hung on every available pole in the area." Ten 10,000-lumen lights were hung, an example of the relatively autonomous actions performed by a public utility under such circumstances without prior request or consultation with the city director of public works, who is in charge of street lighting. Telephone poles were used for lighting purposes without prior clearance from Southwestern Bell, and no one dreamed for a moment of consulting the ordinances approved by the Wichita City Commission to determine the magnitude of street lighting within the city (three 2,500-lumen lights for the area in which the utility installed ten 10,000-lumen lights). This was accomplished by a crew of about ten men between the hours of 2:00 and 7:00 P.M. This illumination was augmented by portable lighting which formed a regular part of the equipment of the public units responding to the crash. When the illumination was later cut back to the three 2,500-lumen lamps local residents complained ("That was probably the best lit hole-in-the-ground in the city," one K.G. and E. man exclaimed), and it was necessary to explain the technicality that street-lighting provided by a public utility must normally conform to the amount stipulated by city ordinance.

While electricity had been restored to all inhabited houses in the crash area, scores remained without gas, and would be without it for days. A K.G. and E. official, Wilson Cadman, on George Weckel's staff, went to work rounding up portable electric heaters to serve the minimal needs of the affected homes. The utility had a few heaters of its own on display. With help from the Red Cross and any source offering it, about 160 portable heaters were gathered from local stores and distributors and loaned to families. The utility took responsibility for distributing these, gathering them, and returning them to their owners after the need for them had abated. Officials received no complaints from the owners about the care of the heaters, nor did anyone fail to return them.

In a situation of this kind there is the problem of cost—if a private business with a profit orientation cares to define it as a problem. Who pays the bill when a private entrepreneurial/public utility responds to emergency? The portable heaters, for example, provided inadequate heat at a cost substantially higher than that of a normal electric heating system. Was it a sense of civic responsibility, good public relations, or plain instinct which led the electric utility to underwrite one-half of the increased monthly utility bill attributable to the heaters? Speculation on motives, by a third party, would probably be as fruitless as introspection by those who made the decision. Did the utility earn friends or gain enemies in collecting, distributing, and reclaiming the heaters and in sharing the cost of the heating? None of the officials interviewed recalled any complaints. The final answer to the question, "Who pays the bill?" seems to be that the cost of emergency service is a part of doing business for a public utility. To put it in the words of a business executive, "We can't . . . send a bill unless we've got a contract and there wasn't any contract in this case except just taking it out and installing it. We didn't try to collect."

We have mentioned the polar extremes of a national military emergency or the crash of a plane, and perhaps a simple house fire. This is a gross oversimplification of the various kinds and magnitudes of emergencies to which "businesses affected with a public interest," to use legal terminology, may respond. Under a mutual assistance pact with neighboring utilities, K.G. and E. responds to emergencies which exceed the capabilities of a single company. Such was the case when a tornado devastated Topeka in 1966. K.G. and E. in Wichita initially provided standby service for Hutchinson, Salina, and other communities served by the Topeka utility, so that Topeka could safely put all of its crews and equipment into the disaster area, and later, when damages had been assessed and the nature of the work to be done clarified, Wichita sent crews directly into Topeka to help restore service.

Gold Cross Ambulance Service

Ambulance service is a rather chancy business, but there are those who seem to like it and who can survive financially. "We render the service first and then try to attempt collection from the patient if it is possible," says Kenneth Thompson, describing the basic economics of the business. Thompson operates Gold Cross Ambulance Service in Wichita, Kansas. "We do have a contract with the City of Wichita that pays for no-pickups, when they call us on an accident or something that involves the police department, if we go there and the ambulance isn't needed; then the city pays us a dry-run fee of half our regular fare. But if we pick up a patient, then it is our responsibility to collect from the patient."

Thompson reports that in other areas in Kansas and across the country, most private ambulance services under city or county jurisdictions have contracts providing for the city or county to pay if the company is unable to collect a bill at the end of sixty or ninety days—this is based on the theory that a large portion of ambulance service rendered is for public necessity. In some jurisdictions, of course, ambulance service is a subsidiary activity of police departments or public hospitals.

Thompson reports a 20 per cent write-off each month in Wichita, which is a high price for providing a public service. As president of the Kansas Ambulance Association and a member of the board of directors of the Ambulance Association of America, he speaks with authority on the economics and the technics of ambulance service.

Wichita has had a private ambulance firm only since 1958. It has been the custom in Kansas, as in many states and localities, to depend upon funeral homes to provide ambulance service. Experience with this practice has been unsatisfactory to morticians as well as to the communities concerned. Although the functions of carrying the maimed and the dead may seem to be related, on superficial analysis, morticians generally have a certain expertise and a consequent "mental fix" somewhat different from that of the entrepreneur or public servant. Service can be problematic. If a rotation system is attempted, there may be a large number of morticians among whom to distribute assignments; other problems may arise when a mortician has men and equipment occupied with a funeral and is unable to respond, necessitating further calls and delay. Furthermore, ambulance service is not a profitable sideline for a mortician's business.

In the spring of 1958, the funeral directors of Wichita decided to abandon the ambulance business, and the incorporators of Gold Cross entered into a contract with the funeral directors to take over that service. In December of 1958, Gold Cross was launched, and the city enacted an ambulance ordinance governing all ambulance service in Wichita, requiring permits of convenience and necessity for each ambulance unit; governing the licensing, testing, and qualifications of ambulance teams; and providing for routine physical examinations, vehicle inspection, and minimum liability insurance.

The eighteen ambulances formerly operated by funeral directors were reduced to seven under Gold Cross, and Thompson took charge. It was a natural for him: in effect he had been brought up in the business. "I was brought up in a funeral home in Oklahoma. Actually, my dad was in the funeral business when I was very young and so I've been in a service allied to ambulance service all my life. I worked for an ambulance service in Oklahoma City for a couple of years prior to coming up here in '58 when this corporation was founded."

In 1959, Metropolitan Ambulance Service was founded, receiving two certificates of convenience and necessity from the city. Thereupon two were removed from Gold Cross, thus keeping the total number of ambulances to seven. The police rotate ambulance calls coming to them according to the number of ambulances operated by each company. Each company keeps a spare vehicle which can be used in areas where city regulations are not operative, or in the event of disaster.

Thompson did not know that the Airport Disaster Committee even existed until he was called to a December meeting in 1964.

> I went to the Christmas Eve meeting and I had been to one earlier, one previous, in the early part of December, and that was when we were included in the program and became aware of it. At the time, I was delegated the responsibility of trying to ascertain how many vehicles we had that could be immediately used for ambulances in Wichita, without going outside of the city. And then, after determining that number, to go on and see how many we could reasonably expect within a short period of time from outside of Wichita.
>
> Of course, I first started out with the two companies and determined the total number of vehicles that would be available from the two, which totals thirteen that the two firms could put out immediately in the case of a disaster. Then the funeral homes were the next logical step, because they do have vehicles that could be used as ambulances, and from the local funeral homes we have a total of eighteen vehicles which can be used.
>
> Then we went to the post office and they assured us of five vehicles on a twenty-four hour basis that we could get any time it was necessary, plus a limited additional number of vehicles if it was determined they were needed. Then we went to the Wichita Chapter of the National Defense Transportation Committee, who said that they would have vehicles available.

> I don't have the exact figure handy right now, but in the neighborhood of forty vehicles in Wichita that we could get immediately, and this doesn't include any of the used car lots who volunteered their station wagons with drivers. It doesn't include the civilians that in any type of disaster you're going to have a lot of volunteers that you can't really put down on paper and plan for. You don't know how many there actually will be, but there will be some. This was forty actual vehicles that we knew we could get immediately.

His responsibilities were to inventory emergency vehicles available in time of disaster, and also to share in the communications function of alerting other concerned groups.

> The mechanics for notifying all of the medical groups are that we [at Gold Cross] will receive the initial call, presumably from the Police Department or the Sheriff's dispatcher, depending on where the disaster has occurred. At the same time that we're notified that it is a disaster, which again is sometimes hard to determine, because the tornado hit one of the more well-to-do parts of town we had, it wasn't considered a disaster until it was over with. [The tornado September 3, 1966, caused extensive damage but no loss of life in the northeast quadrant, east of Hillside, the nominal division line between the Negro section and the white.] But the mechanics would be that we would receive the call, all of our units would be immediately dispatched. All of Metropolitan's units would be immediately dispatched. Then our dispatchers would start the pyramid system of calling out the other units as we determine that more units are necessary. The Red Cross would be notified at the same time we're notified. We wouldn't have to call them. But my dispatchers will notify the funeral homes and the post office and the National Defense Transportation Committee. And then we'll go from there, depending upon the nature of the disaster and the need. But with having forty right here in town, presuming that most of them would be operative and that we could get

them, we can move eighty and possibly ninety to ninety-five patients without getting additional equipment.

Also, our dispatcher has the responsibility of notifying all of the hospital emergency rooms because we have direct phones to each one of the emergency rooms. We've got the best communications system for that phase of it. We notify the hospital emergency rooms and advise them that there has been a disaster and try to keep them posted from time to time as it progresses. And also, we notify the medical society, who at that time, depending on the type of disaster, where it is, will either notify their disaster teams to go to the scene or to go to the hospitals. If it's an air crash, well they have their air disaster teams of which part of them would go to the scene of the accident, and additional doctors would be summoned to the hospital. If it is a large casualty situation where there would be fifty, seventy-five, one hundred or more patients at a scene there would be several doctors sent out there to act as sorters to triage the patients so that they can be sorted as to those that should be taken to the hospital immediately and those that can wait. [Thompson defines "triage" in this way: "They don't treat the patients, they only examine them and determine if it is a minor situation, a serious situation, or one that is a fatality, or will probably be a fatality. So the minor ones will be moved to the hospital later, the serious ones will go immediately. Those that are fatalities, or probably will be, will not ordinarily be moved."]

Explaining the logic behind the assignment of such a heavy communication responsibility to a private entrepreneur (and here we could get into a lengthy digression on the appropriateness of the popular "private-public" dichotomy with respect to the performance of social functions), he responds simply: "Well, it is [a heavy responsibility], but we have the best communication system available for notifying these particular people and that's why I actually volunteered. The police department has an extremely long list of people that they have to notify. The fire department will get most of the citizens' calls. We get quite a few of them, but our dispatchers would have a little bit more free time to get this done. It doesn't take too long. We've got it set up on a pyramid system, so we only have to make a few phone calls and then somebody else makes the rest of them."

Saturday is generally clean-up day at Gold Cross. It is normally a light day for ambulance service, since surgery is seldom scheduled and many doctors' offices are closed. "Our primary business on the weekends is generally emergency calls. So, generally Saturday around here is devoted to clean-up day, and that's what we were in the process of doing when the plane crashed on the 16th."

Gold Cross, like many participants responding to the crash, received their first news on a radio broadcast which reported that some type of plane—"the first reports that I had was that it was a single engine plane"—was down in the northeast part of the city. The first call to the area came from the police and directed an ambulance to report to 2033 North Ash, one block east of Piatt. This came in at 9:45 A.M.

> I took the call myself, primarily, really, to see what had happened and we knew that it was in the area of the plane crash. The information that we got from the police dispatcher didn't indicate that this was concerned with the plane crash. We try to refrain from calling the Police Department or the Fire Department when we know something has happened. We know that they'll call us if they need us. Their switchboard lights up like a Christmas tree anytime anything happens in town. So we don't bother them. We wait until they call us before we go.
>
> When I got in the area up there and attempted to find the address, I could see that it was more than just a single engine plane had crashed. So I radioed back for them to check with the dispatcher and see what the situation was . . . and to start some more units up in the area. Actually the call on North Ash where I was originally dispatched was a no-pickup. The patient was already gone.

Thompson called for all of his remaining units, and meanwhile the police dispatcher had notified Metropolitan while Gold Cross, according to Thompson, had notified the hospitals and the Medical Society.

Thompson moved from Ash to the south end of the fire area, where the initial command post had been set up. There he found police Colonel Fraipont. Shortly after Thompson moved to the new command post at the vacant lot at 21st and Piatt, where he found McGaughey and Pond. "By that time we had determined there wasn't going to be a need for a great number of ambulances . . . but all the ones that were there stayed . . . and we had one standing to the south of the fire on Seventeenth."

In effect, the crash was anticlimactic for the ambulance men. One "MV-Ped" (motor-vehicle, pedestrian accident) took Ambulance 14 off the scene and, to Thompson's best recollection, about four injured persons were taken to hospitals by ambulance. The ambulance attendants had little occasion to work with the doctors on the site, who were "primarily pathologists and coroners." They did help with the removal of tagged bodies to the health department's improvised morgue; indeed this turned out to be their principal function.

Anticlimactic or not, Thompson feels that the crash exemplified the value of advanced planning.

> It was well-coordinated as far as each department that was there knew what their job was and knew what the other departments were doing, so that there wasn't a lot of wasted time as to who's going to do this and who's going to do that, and who's in charge. Our meetings at the Airport with the Disaster Committee had set up the ground rules very well, and, as I said earlier, the first thing that I did when I saw how bad it was, was to find the command post. Now if that had happened in '64, I wouldn't even have known there was going to be a command post established; I would have just tried to find somebody that had on enough stars or brass there that looked like he was in charge. But I knew that by being a part of the Committee and attending the meet-

> ings, that in the event of a disaster, if in the city, the Police Department and the Fire Department are to establish a command post from which all communications and orders are to be given. And if it were in the county, it would be the Sheriff's Office and the County Fire Department that would be in charge.

All the bodies had been transported to the morgue by about 2:30 P.M., at which time the number of ambulances on standby at the scene was cut to two until 7:00 P.M. and to one from that point until 10:00 A.M. Sunday morning.

We have stressed earlier that Gold Cross and Metropolitan are private entrepreneurial organizations, organized, in theory at least, to make a profit. Thompson was asked about the problem of cost recovery in a case like this. Each of the victims transported was billed—although payment is tied up in the litigation resulting from the crash. The estates of the dead have been billed and a claim for standby time filed with the Air Force. All this might seem callous on a casual reading, but the sharing of costs is a serious question for private entreprenuers who have an obligation to respond in disasters, yet must defray their short-term costs such as salaries within a matter of days or weeks. To the suggestion that "a couple of more disasters like this could be disastrous for you," Thompson merely laughed fatalistically and said, "We're attempting to get that straightened out." His work with the Ambulance Association of America, incidentally, has led him to the conclusion that "private ambulance services are generally either left out or are one of the last ones that are considered when plans are being developed for coordinating response to potential disaster."

The Red Cross

Tom Irving, director of the Sedgwick County Chapter of the American Red Cross, was driving west on 13th Street when the aircraft passed over him. "Not realizing the aircraft was in any kind of trouble, I did see it jettisoning fuel, which I interpreted as being an unusual amount of condensation of moisture in the air. Often you see vapor trails, so I didn't think anything of this. Well, as I got down on Thirteenth, I would guess just before Hillside, a second aircraft of the same make, B-52 model aircraft, came over, brightly orange color, you know, so I recognized it as a military aircraft. And it went on over, and about that time I saw this huge fireball and smoke and I recognized that something had either exploded on the ground or something of the nature of an airplane disaster had occurred."

Instead of heading directly for the scene, Irving drove to the Red Cross office downtown. In view of the early morning coolness, it seemed sensible to pack the station wagon with eight cartons of blankets with which to cover the injured and dead. Pat Kelly, disaster chairman for the Red Cross and a Wichita attorney, had independently learned of the crash from his secretary, who had been listening to the radio. He had also received a call from Irving asking him to man Red Cross headquarters while Irving and Harris Burton, director of safety services, who happened to be in the building, drove to the disaster scene.

When they arrived, Chief McGaughey, Deputy Chief Simpson, and Chief Pond were already on the job. A number of ambulances had already arrived. The Red Cross found it unnecessary to call any of its emergency mobile communications facilities to the scene, since the divisional manager of the telephone company was already there with a telephone in his car, and Colonel Trask of the Air Force had similar equipment. The chief of the Red Cross nursing service, who lived nearby, arrived at the scene, and according to Irving, they concentrated on aiding Dr. Leon Bauman, Wichita-Sedgwick County Director of Public Health, and his chief nurse, to set up a temporary morgue at the command site and to identify remains. The coroner Dr. R. M. Daniels arrived, and it was decided to set up a morgue at the city-county health department building on 9th Street. There the bodies were arranged in a large auditorium, and medical specialists and dentists attempted to help confirm identification of the bodies.

Meanwhile, back at headquarters, Pat Kelly was alerting the chairmen of Red Cross subcommittees in charge of food, shelter, clothing, medical nursing, transportation, and communications, who proceeded to establish their sections and to ready for action. "In addition, we needed volunteers, nurses, both at the scene and out at the morgue. And identification began when families began arriving. Obviously we needed to have people there to comfort them."

A mobile cooking unit was dispatched to the scene, and a nearby school opened to receive the homeless. The school was closed about noon, by which time the dead had been evacuated, the injured were in the hospitals, and the homeless had melted away into the community, to be sheltered by friends and relatives.

Although the school was thus not needed, as it turned out, perhaps the more important fact was that the Red Cross had "earmarked every location in the city, complete with what kind of facility is in it, can they serve food, how many toilets they have in it, even down to how many they can sleep in it and so on. So this school was opened because we knew that in this section the gas had been shut off and these homes were going to get cold pretty soon, and the people were going to begin suffering, so we opened the shelter to relieve them." It seemed at that point, with utilities cut off in a wide area around 20th and Piatt, that housing, feeding, and sleeping a few hundred people might prove a major problem that evening. The precautions taken were sensible and in accordance with manual instructions. However, restoration of electricity in the immediate area and the volunteering of some two hundred electric heaters for temporary use enabled neighborhood residents to remain in their homes in relative comfort.

When the Air Force claims office had been set up, the Red Cross performed a complementary function. Despite tragic circumstances, the government must demand proof of identity and property ownership before it can advance partial payment on a claim, and it can deal only with the next of kin in case of death. When government red tape delayed reasonably quick action, the Red Cross filled in, according to Irving. It gave money, food, and drugs, and guaranteed payment of hospital bills. Because some next-of-kin lived in other states and had no means to get to Wichita, the Red Cross advanced funds for travel.

Providing housing was a touchy problem. Some Negroes, hoping the need for emergency housing might break down housing restrictions in white neighborhoods, felt that efforts at rehousing those in need were restricted to finding houses only in the ghetto. The Red Cross, seeking to escape involvement in a fair-housing crusade in the midst of a disaster, finally offered the few who required housing cash for rent and help in locating a place to live. An advisory committee concluded that $90 per month would be a reasonable rental allowance, and this became standard.

Ad hoc committees proliferate in response to any disaster. The gap between what some committees promise and what they deliver may be extensive, and may contribute to disillusionment upon the part of disaster victims. The January 18 edition of the *Wichita Eagle* announced formation of a Volunteer Disaster Committee, composed of local businessmen and spearheaded by a builder and realtor who acted as chairman. The purpose of the group, which expected donation of "considerable labor and material," was "to repair the damaged homes wherever possible and arrange through the Veterans Administration and Federal Housing Administration housing for those whose homes were destroyed. . . . Committee members explained that by a 'liveable' home they meant one complete with furniture."[3] The committee and its efforts were quickly consigned to oblivion but not before contributing to prevalent misconceptions which exacerbated the problems of a somewhat uneasy group of predominantly white relief workers attempting to help victims most of whom were Negro. As far as can be ascertained, the committee housed none of the victims. Rumors abounded concerning the allegedly untenantable condition of the houses shown by the committee and the committee's supposed policy of offering only houses located in the ghetto. The committee was mistakenly identified with the Red Cross by many persons and it consequently received much blame for the resulting confusion.

Many continue to insist, probably quite correctly, that had the disaster occurred in a white community, affected families would have gone as a matter of course to motels and the Air Force or insurance companies would have picked up the tab. In fairness, however, it must be said that the needy just seemed to be absorbed into the local community, taken in by relatives, neighbors, and friends. Perhaps we are talking not so much about discrimination as we are about the varying pattern of mores of two distinct ethnic groups of different socio-economic status.

Clothing needs were attended to by Operation Holiday, operated from the old courthouse (standing across from the new skyscraper courthouse at Central and Main) and supported by various United Fund agencies. The Red Cross, while making money immediately available for drugs and food, would dispatch applicants to the courthouse for needed clothing. Here, again, there was some disappointment or sense of being short-changed, for the applicants inevitably found only cast-off garments, available in various states of repair or disrepair, odd sizes, and an abundance of some and shortage of other kinds of clothing. Many had imagined they would receive a chit to be honored at a clothing store downtown. Perhaps, again, had the crash occurred in a more affluent, white neighborhood, the victims would have gone to one of the large department stores to buy needed clothing, using available credit, and then filing a claim with the Air Force or insurance company. This was not such a neighborhood.

The point is that there were *distinctions* in treatment and behavior because of the type of neighborhood in which the plane went down. It is yet to be demonstrated, and is alleged by but few, that these were *invidious* distinctions *based upon race*. But it is equally true that if the Negro were not compelled to live in one area, the northeast quadrant of the city, there would not have been a concentration of people of lower socio-economic status in a Negro housing area into which a tanker could crash, spewing death and mayhem as its fuel enveloped the houses in the path of its trajectory. This fact will always remain in the minds of many who live in that northeast area.

Reporting to the regional office of the Red Cross located in St. Louis, Irving stated that twelve houses were totally destroyed, twenty-three had major damage, and sixty-eight had minor damage. He then thought there had been twenty-nine persons killed. This was a situation which he thought the local chapter was well prepared to handle—or rather, participate in handling—both in terms of personnel and funds ("We had a very successful United Fund drive last fall."). Emergency reserves of the Sedgwick County Red Cross were not depleted during the disaster, since, among the *ad hoc* activities carried on independently when word of the crash spread, there was an appeal by TV station KAKE which yielded funds to aid the victims. These funds were deposited in the Fourth National Bank and disbursed at the discretion of a committee. Without going into the details of this operation, suffice it to say that by mid-April, 1965, the Red Cross reported a disaster expenditure of $6,992.03; the Fourth National Bank fund of $6,273.75 was, by vote of the committee, transferred to the Sedgwick County Red Cross. Other miscellaneous contributions had been made directly to the Red Cross.

A degree of impersonality is unavoidable in any effort of an institutional nature. There are questions to be asked, forms to be filled out and officials to whom the professionals on the spot are accountable for their actions and expenditures. It is inevitable, therefore, that such an operation will be rewarded for its efforts as often with brickbats as with corsages. Who, for example, is grateful to a county welfare department? The taxpayers generally are suspicious of the efficiency of the operation and the recipients resentful because needs are not being met more fully. Such feelings were expressed by a Negro who said, "The Red Cross naturally is an agency which collects thousands of dollars a year on a very logical appeal to a person's emotions, sense of decency, and sense of wanting to help someone else. In many instances those things that they announce in practicality, their practices never come to their announcements." Another Negro said, "I don't think the Red Cross performed to the degree that they possibly could perform for the type of contributions they got." The latter commentator was also of the opinion that much of the money contributed "filtered out into higher salaries."

More flexible than the Air Force and freer to dispense funds and aid without prior approval from regional headquarters, the Red Cross remains a bureaucratic organization—employing that term in a non-pejorative sense—an organization of professionals. In Wichita, until after the crash, a Negro had never sat on its board. Certainly there was apprehension and uneasiness on the part of many of the Negro victims who—as they saw it—were buffeted from one set of interrogators, the Air Force, to another, the Red Cross, when all they wanted was immediate help with no questions asked.

The Sedgwick County Red Cross was not insensitive to these problems—witness the subsequent appointment of Jim Garmon, a Negro, to its board. It is interesting to note, however, that while all participants praised the preplanning of the Disaster Committee generally, Chiefs Pond and McGaughey were anxious to emphasize, on a *post hoc* assessment of their participation in the disaster, the areas in which they had gone wrong and the changes they would make next time. The Red Cross higher echelon, on the other hand, concluded at a post-disaster luncheon meeting that there was nothing that they would do differently, could they repeat their disaster experience.

The Salvation Army

Captain Raymond L. Wert of the Salvation Army came to Wichita about two years before the KC-135 crash from South Bend, Indiana, where he had been commanding officer for the city. Of Pennsylvania Dutch and Evangelical Reform background, Wert had been in the merchant marine before World War II, and he found the Salvation Army through street-corner experiences while at Great Lakes Navy Training Station during the War. He and Mrs. Wert, a descendant of the Quaker preacher Mary Moon, who converted Herbert Hoover to the faith, lived with their three daughters in the west part of Wichita. Here he commanded the Wichita West Side Salvation Army, comprised of a recreation center and church.

The Army is divided into four territories in the U.S.: Eastern, Central, Western, and Southern. According to Captain Wert, more than 10 per cent of the cadets in training in the Chicago training school are Negroes, and the Army there has at least two large corps, largely Negro-staffed, which serve Negroes. Thus he was not going to strange or alien territory when he entered what is popularly called the ghetto in Wichita on the morning of January 16, 1965. "We have a statement from our national commander and the Salvation Army General in London that if anyone ever refuses service to anyone because of race, color, or creed, then this is an infraction of what we would call the papal bull, so to speak. And not only that, the Salvation Army was born in the throes of a social war. The Army has always tried to stand up for what was right, tried to take its stand. At our corps in west Wichita we have no colored, we have some Mexican. Downtown has some Mexican and colored.

But the north side, of course, I think they have some colored there. We have four corps in this city. We have a home and hospital here."

Captain Wert was asked about the Army's creed and how it could lead to participation in the alleviation of distress in a disaster situation:

Q. You tend to deal with people who don't relate to other people?

A. Yes, this is true. The Army has always felt that . . . Booth's idea was this, that if we're to lift the level of society, Professor, we must, as good real-estate men know, if you have a bad piece of property in an area you don't dress up all the other pieces, you go to the man in the area and you tell him, "Why don't you fix your property up, can we help you?" And in turn the whole area's property values go up. So Booth believed that if you want to lift the bottom you don't stretch the middle and top. His premise was that you push the bottom up higher and as a consequence the whole level of society is then pushed up higher. When William Booth was told to give a command for his officers, he said, "Go for souls and go for the worst." He said, "Strain the very sewers, net the very sewers for men. Keep them from going down the drain." And I think that's a good premise for the Army.

Q. Well, now, how does this get you into emergency type of work? I mean, if I had a fire in my house, there's nothing about my socio-economic status which would interest the Salvation Army in me. But apparently you would be interested.

A. Right. Well, it represents to us a loss to a man, the property that means something to that person. The very fact that someone's concerned about them—we're not going to work on their "socio-economic" that's for sure. We believe that if we go and render a service to them, he knows we're there. This is the basic premise and secondly we can render an effective service . . . . Of course, men that are out working always neglect their own personal needs, you understand, we serve them. And you understand that in a large disaster many people are displaced; their homes are displaced. They are displaced. . . . The Salvation Army feels that if we get in there, we can get a little of our religion, so to speak, in. And show them that we are concerned about them. The Army believes that we empathize with them in this respect, that we can help them. . . . Before you can talk with some people, you must of necessity sometimes feed their stomach first too. You can't tell a man about a loving God, when he's got an empty stomach—he'll tell you to go you know where. It's like, remember when Cardinal Cushing said, the man was dying and he said, "Do you believe in the Father, the Son, and the Holy Ghost?" The man said, "Have you started a quiz program?" But you cannot tell a man about a loving God who cares for a person when he hasn't got two cents to rub together. I mean that, how can you tell them? I don't see how you can. Here's a man who hasn't a shirt on his back, who has six kids at home and he doesn't have a job. You tell him about the love of God, and he'll tell you who the so and so cares about me. Now we felt that if we went up there, we could render a service to the area (this is our contention). We could help to alleviate the present needs of the personnel involved in clearing the area, and we could make an impression upon the people, so to speak.

I was able to render a spiritual service as a minister. I was able to talk to Mr. Brown, remember that fellow that came screaming across there looking for that family. I was able to calm him down and talk to him about spiritual things. I said, "These people are gone—you've got to admit it, there in that house, they're gone." And I was able to render . . . . The very impression that the Salvation Army uniform was there, people came up and talked to me and tell me things, which, people have confidence in the Army. I would say that was another reason we were there perhaps to render at the time of need. I was not able to counsel anyone who had a lost loved one. I was not able to do that. They were taken already out of the area. And those were at the hospital in shock and their minister was already there.

I was struck by the fact that none of these people were around there. Either they were gone—dead, or they were gone from the area already. They were gone before we . . . I never saw them. We were down there within twenty minutes. But I never saw anyone that was in that area. I don't know how they got them out of there so fast. Everybody must have run, because the shock was so great that they first left the area. And then after the explosion, they started coming back. The explosion then the implosion of human people coming into the area.

The Salvation Army is directly informed of all two or more alarm fires by the fire department. It is accustomed to working with the fire department, in particular, and is as much oriented toward providing sustenance for firemen on duty at such fires as it is toward succoring the individuals and families displaced by them. Thus there exists a tendency on the part of firemen to talk more of the Salvation Army than of the Red Cross and other relief organizations operating in Wichita. On this occasion, Wert arrived on the scene with a truck and coffee and doughnuts. He had not had previous contact with the Disaster Committee, but had rolled upon receiving a telephone call from John Hudson, corps treasurer, and a follow-up fire department call, both alerting him to a plane crash in the northeast part of the city. These came in at about 9:40 A.M.

Upon instructions from Chief McGaughey, to whom he went as a matter of course, Captain Wert set up his canteen at the north end of the fire, away from but near the command area. From Saturday morning at 10:00 until the following Friday afternoon at 4:30 P.M., the Army was present—a total of six days and six hours—taking care of the food needs of official personnel working in the disaster area and of some needy residents. Additional equipment and help arrived shortly after the canteen was first set up.

The magnitude of the disaster was overawing at first: "I had no comprehension at all of the immensity of it. I didn't realize the . . . what I'd need when I got there. I'd never seen a plane crash spewing things like that all over the place. I was sickened by the smell. I mean, I recall the smell (of course, that fuel itself didn't help any, and then the foam itself hitting the fire—I'd never seen foam quite like that), but I was amazed at the effectiveness of the firemen. I was struck by, when they came across a dead body. I was struck by that, you could hear a pin drop, the men may have been joking and talking about each other, but when they came to a dead body, it was so quiet and so hushed. Nobody spoke."

Soon discerning that they would be present for a long time, Captain Wert arranged with local grocers to purchase large quantities of food on a chit basis. Razook's, a supermarket located within a few hundred yards of the point of impact and which had lost considerable plate glass (not to mention customer equilibrium) as a result of the shock wave from the crash, was a likely source of supplies. According to Wert, it is customary under such circumstances for a Salvation Army officer to walk into a grocery or dry goods store and receive credit to the extent of hundreds or thousands of dollars, on a chit-signing basis. The immediate impact of disaster, and the image which is enjoyed by groups like the Salvation Army and Red Cross, apparently combine to overcome normal qualms which one might expect of a storekeeper witnessing the depletion of his stock without a concomitant increase of register totals. "No problem at all. I just sign tickets. I went around and collected bills and gave them in. Some disasters—I know that in the disaster in Udall, Salvation Army officials just went into a store and bought $10,000 worth of clothes right off the collar—just signed for them. They just accept the Army's word—that's it."

By Wert's calculation, the Army at the time of the crash had facilities which could be used to house as many as two hundred or more families on a temporary basis. Housing, of course, turned out to be the least of the worries in connection with this disaster. Most of those deprived of houses had been incinerated with their dwellings.

Asked about his relationship with the Red Cross, Captain Wert told of attending an Office of Civil Defense management school at Battle Creek, Michigan, and of his understanding, on the basis of that experience, that a national plan exists providing for the inter-relating of the two organizations. At the Wichita level, he had met Red Cross Director Tom Irving once or twice, and he understood that the Army brigadier in charge of Wichita operations saw him more frequently. The Army had not been included in previous Wichita community disaster planning, and, by Captain Wert's testimony, had at the most a loose relationship with the Red Cross. On the other hand, Tom Irving came close to expressing resentment of the Salvation Army's disaster participation which, it seemed to the interviewer, he regarded at best as redundant of Red Cross activity and at worst as a transgression on Red Cross jurisdiction.

This account of the Salvation Army's response to the crash is based upon an interview with Captain Wert, who wrote these comments on his experiences of January 16:

> DISASTER—1965
>
> At 9:40 A.M., January 16, 1965, the telephone rang in my office at The Salvation Army, 2151 W. Dora St., Wichita, Kansas. The call was from our Corps Treasurer, John Hudson, informing me that a plane had crashed in the northeast section the city. I put down the phone rather hurriedly; ran out of my office and looked toward the northeast and saw, to my dismay, a dark, angry-looking black cloud slowly spreading itself across Wichita like a black pall. In horror, I turned, retraced my steps to the phone and told Pete to get ready to go out on Disaster Service, Mr. Hudson being EM in charge of Manpower for this very service. I called my wife from a meeting of the Junior Soldiers and informed her of the situation; telling her that I would be out for awhile. Little did I know then that I would be on duty for six (6) full days serving the needs of men engaged in rescue and fire-fighting. As soon as I reached my car and turned on the ignition, I switched on my CB Radio, and Bill Baughman was on the air trying to round up the units of SAC (Salvation Army Communications) to assist us at the scene of the disaster. The time was now 9:50 A.M. I was then appraised of the exact

location of the accident and was told that the plane had gone down in the area of 20th and Piatt. I proceeded to the scene, meanwhile listening to the disaster preparedness made by the leader of the SAC group who had switched to Channel 5, using the call letters, 17W4878, which had been assigned to The Salvation Army, and arrived there at 10:10 A.M. I met Bill Baughman, who told me that the canteen was on its way. We walked up close to the actual impact area and saw a scene that will forever live in my memory. Imagine the very pits of hell opening up; revealing intense heat, fire and brimstone escaping and engulfing everything in its path. The smell was such as to make the heartiest man shrink and hold his nose. Firemen were everywhere, hoses were spewing their trails of water and foam causing great clouds of smoke to ascend in the air. We saw Chief McGaughey, with four (4) or five (5) of the assistant chiefs engaged in directing the efforts of the valiant men of the Fire Department. I was struck by the calmness of Chief McGaughey, who directed his assistants here and there holding the spread of flames to a minimum. CD Heavy Rescue were there, Sheriff's Reserves were there, the Sheriff's Department were there directed by Sheriff Vern Miller; the City Police were there, under the able direction of Chief Pond. The Air Police, under the direction of Major Joseph Lynn, were there starting to draw a cordon around the area allowing none to enter except those on official business. They were to be commended for their fine display of calmness in the face of a rather charged situation; asking people to move back very calmly and kindly.

(We are now a unified command; I will speak in the collective pronoun.)

We then requested permission to move our Canteen Bus (which, by then, had arrived on the scene) farther into the area to better serve the needs of the men. Permission was quickly granted and we moved up Piatt Street and parked on the east side of Piatt Street directly opposite the conflagration. We served both from the bus and from across the street by using portable coffee containers and served coffee, donuts, sandwiches and cold water to one and all. After the fire had subsided slightly we moved right up into the impact area to better facilitate serving the needs of the men. The Air Police, having set up their headquarters in tents and the Air Force setting up their Command Post in a nearby building, it was decided that we move our mobile Canteen setup adjacent to the Air Police tent and in close proximity to the Command Post. Accordingly, we moved our vehicle around the block and parked our bus one-half block south of 21st Street on Piatt. Colonel James Trask, the Base Commander for McConnell AFB gave us the necessary permission to acquire the space to function to the best advantage. Major Lynn, the CO of the Air Police, gave us permission to use part of the Air Police because of the cold weather and the light situation. This offer was readily accepted. By this time, Mac Findly, of the Sedgwick County Mobile Home Dealer's Association, arrived on the scene with an office trailer to use as a rest area and as a command post for the Communications unit. On Sunday, it was ascertained that we would be there at least four (4) or five (5) more days and that we would need supplies. A plea for supplies was issued via the TV stations and Radio Stations at 3:00 P.M., Sunday, January 17, 1965. The response was so overwhelming, so much was given that we had to ask the TV and Radio media to discontinue our distress call at 5:30 P.M., Sunday, January 17, 1965. So many people came direct to the disaster area, bringing their donations, that they were blocking the streets. All in all, the people of Wichita donated over nine (9) tons of foodstuffs; including: Canned goods, bread, donuts, chili, hot chocolate, coffee, cakes, pies, milk, orange juice, soups, cups, napkins, etc., ad infinitum. One lady baked over forty (40) pies individually and sent them in. She also made home-made chicken noodle soup, that was "out of this world." She also baked approximately 10 chickens for the men. Needless to say, foregoing items were disposed of summarily. The woman's name is: Mrs. Wm. Wilder, 3845 N. Clarence and she deserves of big vote of thanks. We continued serving both night and day until Friday, January 22, 1965, when the Air Police were secured and the City Police took over jurisdiction. The SAC unit were my right arm; and without their assistance we could not have operated as efficiently as we did. Mr. Bill Baughman, Civilian Director of the Wichita Area for the Salvation Army, and Mr. Bob Nofsinger, Assistant Civilian Director for the Wichita Area for the Salvation Army CD, were there ready to assist whenever and wherever needed and they deserve a vote of thanks. All of the SAC members were involved in this most important service. The local business houses were more than generous in donating items to be used. It would be impossible to name them all for fear of forgetting someone and offending them. Units of The Salvation Army were there namely: El Dorado, under the direction of Lt. David Doty; Newton, under the direction of Lt. Herbert Dahl; Arkansas City, under the direction of Captain Bruce Tewautz; Wichita #1 (Citadel) Corps, under the direction of Captain Carl Amick; Wichita #2 (North) Corps, under the direction of Auxiliary Captain Charles Shoults; Wichita #3 Corps, under the direction of Major Lonnie Myers (R); Wichita #4 (West Corps), under the direction of Captain Ramon Wert; Booth Memorial Hospital, under the direction of Brigadier Florence Toles; Men's Social Service Center, under the direction of Brigadier Joseph Timberman; City Co-Ordinator's office, under the direction of City Co-Ordinator, Brigadier Nils Bonger. Many other Corps offered their help but it was found that we would now have enough help and their offer was gratefully declined. Captain James Barker, the Director of CD for The Salvation Army in and for the state of Kansas was there to advise and assist us in planning and directing our efforts. All in all, we were able to render the following services: 46,486 cups of coffee were served;

8,764 sandwiches were prepared and served; 5,563 cups of hot chocolate were given out; and 1,528 servings of juice were served; 12,138 bowls of chili were dispensed; 7,338 bowls of soup were served; 165 packs of cookies were given out as were 627 packs of donuts; 75 pies were dispensed and 1,260 pints of milk were served. Besides the above, local residents brought pots and pans to fill to feed their families; being unable to cook because the gas was shut off. The man hours were as follows; SAC—1500; SA—1928; Volunteers—1140. Bringing the total man hours to 4,568 hours. We were secured at 1530, January 22, 1965.

Ramon L. Wert, Captain, S.A.
Area Director for The Salvation
Army Civil Defense Unit

Mennonite Disaster Service

A *Handbook for Mennonite Disaster Service Volunteers,* published in mimeographed form in 1960, speaks of disaster and appropriate responses to it in terms sufficiently simple and succinct to warrant repetition here:

A. Disaster is a great catastrophe, natural or man-made, which leaves many people helpless and suffering
B. Disasters occur in all parts of the world
C. Disasters occur most frequently in April, May, and June
D. Disasters are alike in that they leave the same kind of problems:
    Familiar living patterns disorganized
    Community services disrupted
    People killed or injured
    Families separated
E. Calculated disaster service is the best avenue of service to relieve human suffering.

Vernon R. Wiebe, author of the manual, goes on to identify three basic types of service responsive to disaster: rescue, relief, and rehabilitation. Of the Mennonite Disaster Service, he says, "MDS has improved its contacts, it has often been able to arrive in time for" relief-type work; but this work and rescue work are for the most part left to other public and private agencies. The major contributuion of MDS to a disaster is in the rehabilitation phase.

The Mennonite Disaster Committee traces its origins to the biblical injunctions to help one's neighbors and to reinforce faith with works. Its expansion into a nation-wide organization from its origin in 1950 in Hesston, Kansas, stemmed from repeated demonstrations of its capability to produce men and machinery to help in time of flood, tornado, or other natural or man-made disaster. It also stems from an increasing sense of responsibility to be organized and ready to respond when calls are made upon it. The multiplication of calls for help is indicative not merely of the number of disasters of large or small magnitude which occur in the United States in any given year, but also of appreciation of the spirit and industry which characterize the proffered help. This is, again, best put in the words which Vernon R. Wiebe directed to volunteers in his *Handbook:*

> The attitude in which you work is very important. The MDS volunteer must understand what he is doing and why he is doing it. He has come to work "in the name of Christ." In this spirit the volunteer will be friendly and optimistic. He will be quiet and reserved. No task will be too menial to do. He will be a sympathetic and understanding listener. He will respect personal property and the wishes of its owners. He will pray grace before meals and participate in group devotions. He will watch his language and his habits. And above all, he will be able to give a spiritual account for his service. He has come because he believes that he shall "love the Lord his God with all his heart and his neighbors as himself."

The MDS volunteers share in little of the drama, excitement, and, let it be said, even glamour, attendant upon disaster, insuring a plenitude of spectators as well as workers upon the spot. They will be more likely to come in at the point at which all that remains to be done is the drab, disheartening, and totally undramatic job of cleaning up and laying at least the foundations for reconstruction.

The MDS contact man in Wichita is Rueben Janzen, a quiet-spoken man who acts as the local eyes and ears of John Diller, an originator of the service and still its national coordinator who operates out of his home in Hesston, Kansas. He can mobilize twenty men or two hundred from the surrounding towns, depending upon need, and they travel hundreds of miles to serve. The usual procedure is for "field men" or crew leaders to ascertain the problem and gain official permission to contribute aid. Then the requisite number of volunteers are mustered, equipped with identification which will enable them to pass through security lines, and put to work under direction of their leaders.

Janzen was driving in Wichita on Saturday morning on personal business, when he looked to the northeast and saw "a big black balloon of smoke." Turning on the car radio he heard of the KC-135 crash. He started toward the crash, but upon hearing it was a military plane that was down and that the police requested that persons stay away from the site, he returned home.

> One of my co-workers lives in that area and he tried to get to this place and he could hardly get out of it once he got in. Couple of my friends, one of them was working in an area close to it, and he felt the heat where he was. He was that close to it. They got out, too, because they knew they might be in a position where they could get pinned in with the traffic.
>
> People began to ask why we weren't in there and it wasn't hard to tell that when the military takes over you stay out. So we kept in contact with the people here in town who are the officials: the police, the civil defense, and they finally gave us clearance after they had checked all the people out and cleared all the necessary legal entanglements that were involved.

This was in February, four or five weeks after the crash. Prior to that time, security and legal considerations kept the group from undertaking the cleanup.

Janzen understands that the military secured necessary legal clearance to permit the MDS to complete the demolition of a few of the near-totally destroyed dwellings. With the help of equipment volunteered by a construction company to cart the debris away, while the police directed traffic and the fire department stood by, MDS volunteers from Wichita and from Newton, twenty miles to the north, contributed what they could to rehabilitate a city block which, a month earlier, had been alive but then was a scarred testament to the corrosive power of 50,000 gallons of flaming jet fuel, sprayed from a limping tanker which fell out of the sky at 20th and Piatt.

VI

The People It Touched

Smoke rose through the blanket covering the 21st body.

Stretcher-bearers set the 22nd body down nearby.

The charred flight suit told he had been an airman.

Several doors down the street from the vacant lot "morgue," a small metal stake bearing a tag called attention to a burned body. It was the only evidence that a person had perished amid the rubble of a front room at 2101 North Piatt. The home of Clarence W. Walker was gone, along with whoever had been in it.

Next door, Forrest Crawford talked quietly. He lived alone at 2107. He had been in the hallway, heard an explosion, ran out to find a wall of flames at his right, and escaped unhurt before the fire devoured his house.

Many neighbors were not so lucky.

One body was found in a bathtub. Children were killed—some playing in their yards, some trapped in their rooms.

Atop the rubble in the basement at 2053 were the remains of two young ones.

"Oh, my God!" moaned Joe T. Martin of 2031. His shocked mind was absorbing the deaths of two sons. "I was laying in bed and heard the boys talking. They were getting ready to go someplace. Then I think one ran out the front door and one out the back.

"Someone told me he burnt right there," the father said. The body of either Joe, 25, or Gary Lynn, 17, apparently was the first found. Just outside the door it lay, covered.

"Another blanket over here," called a searcher from a home which had just cooled enough to enter. There was another body to cover.

"Over here, father." And a young Catholic priest moved to offer last rites to an airman, in case the man was of his faith.

And life went on.

Generals and colonels arrived from north and south to probe the tragedy's cause. The Red Cross and Salvation Army served coffee and sandwiches to wet, cold rescue workers.[1]

A community disaster is a montage of personal tragedies linked by time, cause, and contiguity. Newspaper reporters accumulate bits and pieces of experience—the horrifying incident witnessed by an onlooker, the glancing touch with death which leaves the fortuitous survivor with indelible physical or psychic scars. Rev. J. E. Mason was one of the first on the disaster scene. " 'I don't know what family it was. I saw him burn up . . . a little boy . . . running out of the house . . . all curled up in flames,' the grief-stricken minister said." " 'My boy's in there. My boy's in there,' screamed another man being restrained by neighbors." "Sharon Jackson, 10, was getting her sister a drink of water in their house at 1842 Pennsylvania. She looked out the window, saw the diving plane, and 'fell.' Robert Jackson, 12, of 1831 Piatt, saw the plane coming at him. A moment later he was rolling in dirt trying to smother flames on his back."[2]

These are the terms in which Wichitans learned of the personal toll taken by the crash. Interviews conducted in the months following the crash make it possible to reconstruct in somewhat more depth the experiences of persons who were close to the 2000 block of North Piatt that morning and survived, or who were close to some who did not.

Laura Randolph's Story

Laura Randolph left her kindergarten-aged daughter Tracy at the girl's grandmother's house at 2037 Piatt just after 9:00 A.M. Saturday morning. "I asked her if she wanted to take her best doll over to grandma's and she wanted to, so I let her. When I got there my mother and brother and my cousin, and this other man that lived there . . . . Well, the man was up sitting in a chair and my mother was still in bed. She was sleeping in the living room on a pull divan and I knocked on the door and she got up and let me in. She asked me something about a stamp and I said that I didn't have one. Then I asked her not to let Tracy play out that day because it was cool and I had washed her hair and I didn't want her running around."

Mrs. Randolph, divorced, was a student at the Wichita School of Practical Nursing under the Manpower Development and Training Act. She "moonlighted" on Saturdays to supplement the income which she received from the federal government during the period of training. Having left Tracy with the grandmother, Mrs. Randolph proceeded to the Riverside section of Wichita, where she worked as a domestic. The house at 2037 Piatt was virtually at the point of impact.

She was at work in the bathroom when she learned from her employer's son of the crash. "He said, 'Laura, there is a plane down in the 2000 block on Piatt,' and I just started to shake. I went to the telephone and the first number I dialed was her number, and of course the lines were dead. . . . I just left everything. I didn't try to pick up or straighten up. I just got in the car and came as fast as I could but traffic was so heavy coming out 17th street—well, I don't know—it took me thirty or forty minutes to come what would ordinarily take me twenty minutes." She parked at Hydraulic and 17th Streets, some blocks from the crash area and ran to 19th and Minnesota, one block south and west of the crash. "I came by Minnesota because I have a cousin that lives there in that block and I asked him where it was or did they know for sure that it was in our block, but they didn't know at that time. I feel now they knew but they didn't tell me what was down and where it was. They kind of told me that there wasn't any point in my going up there and they kept me there for a little while, and then I went back and got in my car and I drove all the way back up to 13th and back around to get to where I lived because you couldn't come straight through here."

Her sister and grandfather had gone to the crash scene and returned with the feeling, shared by neighbors, that perhaps the family had escaped from the burning house. A series of telephone calls to the hospitals elicited no report on anyone fitting the descriptions she offered. "I didn't make any attempt to go over there anymore and I just walked and we called various people and then we could wait. Everytime the telephone rang just . . . I felt up until . . . I didn't know for certain until . . . well really and truly, I don't really know it now. About 4:00 in the evening when the evening paper came out and of course the paper stated that all the persons that were at this residence had been killed, and they named the people. They didn't get this information from us here. I don't know who they got it from. The postman or neighborhood people—but nobody here identified them in that way."

Because Mrs. Randolph could not bring herself to go to the morgue to which the bodies had been taken, she prevailed upon a close friend to do so. The person who made the trip did not personally see or identify any of the bodies, and Mrs. Randolph says she received no word from any official source that her mother, brother, cousin, and daughter had been killed. On the advice of a friend, she went to the Air Force claims office which had been established in an empty portion of a business building on 21st near Minneapolis, where she was treated "real well." "They explained to us that they were an emergency unit and they were prepared to aid in any immediate need that we might have pertaining to food, shelter, clothing, and of course, as I said this was not my home so I still had food and shelter and clothing, but they said I was entitled to a burial. They advanced us money to make immediate arrangements to bury our family." The same friend suggested that she place her claim in the hands of an attorney, which Mrs. Randolph shortly did.

Mrs. Randolph remained at home for the next week before resuming her practical nurse training. She had completed approximately three-fourths of the course. She reports that she was permitted to fill out the claim for the next Saturday's allowance, which was normal on Monday. However, she was told that since she was no longer the head of a household she could no longer qualify for the weekly allowance under the MDTA training program. Although this decision was challenged with some vehemence by a social worker who had taken an interest in the Randolph case, it remained in effect.

One agency of the federal government thus took the Randolph child's life, depriving the mother of the status of head of household, while another, in consequence of this deprivation, cut off her income. Ultimately, an advance on claims was granted by the Air Force enabling her to complete her training and take the state board examinations for practical nurses. A bit of insurance on Tracy's life helped, also.

The Clarence Walker Story

At the disaster scene, death and survival were the stark alternatives. Few were injured. Fewer still incurred prolonged suffering. One of these few was Clarence Walker, a cook at the Boeing plant, who suffered second and third degree burns and, at the time of a first anniversary newspaper report on the crash, had been hospitalized three times for a total of six weeks. " 'He's a nervous wreck,' Mrs. Walker said—which he charges resulted from the disaster. He maintains he also has a nerve allergy that prevents him from taking showers."[3]

Mr. and Mrs. Walker were interviewed on April 20, 1965, by Frank H. Carpenter and Leonard H. Wesley, Jr., Wichita High School teachers who assisted in the investigations leading to this study: "What happened on the day of the crash; to the best of your ability, would you tell us in your own words?" Mr. Walker answered:

> Me and my wife got up that Saturday morning. Her nephew called us about a pine tree that we brought down from Oklahoma when we went down to bury her father on New Year's. And during our discussion down there we were speaking about pine trees that I couldn't get one to live. And I certainly would like to have one. But they're so expensive up here. I wasn't able to buy one right now. So Mr. Chapman said he had awful good success raising pine trees from down in Oklahoma. See? He would bring them to Kansas and plant them. And

so he brought us one up. That morning he called us about eight o'clock, didn't he? He called us about eight o'clock and ask us how our tree was doing. I told him that it was doing just fine last time I looked out the door. And he asked me when'd I water it last. I said it's eleven degrees out there now and I'm not going out there to water no tree now. I said yes I'm keeping an eye on it because I also have a tree out there that I have from Christmas. Sand in a bucket that I'm trying to root or something like that. So we talked a while. I asked him how his family was getting along. And he said fine.

I went outdoors and got the morning paper; I came in and somehow and some reason we didn't go into the front room at all that morning. We usually go in and turn the TV on and get out trays and look at TV. We didn't have any of the grand-kids or any people at the house beside the boy who stays with us. So my wife asked me had the boy come in yet and I told her, "Yes he came in about four o'clock." And I had gotten up to go to the rest room. He said he didn't have to go to work that day. And could he sleep late. I said, "Why sure—but you'd have to get your own breakfast." He said, "I'd be too glad to do that." So my wife got up and looked in the room to see if he were in there. And immediately she pulled the door back and she sat down and we cooked our breakfast in the kitchen. And we sat down in the kitchen and ate. Oh, I guess it was about quarter to nine. Meantime we had a meeting down to the church at twelve o'clock and it was suppose to last the rest of the evening.

My wife said "I'll start to fix my hair." I said, "Well, I'll go on and get my bath." So I guess about around nine o'clock somewhere, close around that, not looking at the time, I go to the bathroom and run my water—and get out all my clothes, throw them in the clothes hamper and started to get in the tub. And I heard this great commotion. And I heard my wife scream. And she said something like, "The hot water tanker blew up." I immediately rushed out of the bathroom towards the kitchen to see what was wrong with her and when I got out of my bathroom to the kitchen, my living room was boiling with fire. I started into the kitchen. There was so much smoke in the kitchen that I couldn't get through that way; I knew where the backdoor was but didn't know if something was blocking it.

She was fixing her hair, when this plane struck. She immediately got up and rushed out the backdoor. And I was trapped back in the other part of the house. And so, the one thing that I could do—the fire hadn't got back in there yet—it was coming that way and so I started to the bedroom. It was in the living room and it was coming this way, see? That's the reason—it had got in the kitchen, see? Smoke had done filled the kitchen up and had gotten that way—and that little alcove or hallway had cut it off a few seconds and I went in the bathroom and tried to raise the window and couldn't raise the window. Stepped in the tub and I slipped down. I got up again and fell down again. And I said, "Well, I guess this is it." Something said, "Ya got a few more seconds." So I got up from there. I already had this bath thing—this dirty clothes hamper, see? And I started banging on that window. And finally I saw daylight. I didn't take time to pick the glass out. Soon as I saw daylight, I leaped. Immediately after I leaped my backyard was boiling in fire. I fell in the fire. I guess I hadn't got too far from the house before the house had fell in.

Mr. Wesley: What happened to the young man who stayed with you?

Mr. Walker: He was completely demolished.

Mrs. Walker: I don't think he had ever got up, the way they brought him out.

Mr. Walker: The front side of the house. Our house was the first contact. Due to the siding we had on the house, it didn't allow the flame to come in. The only way it could have come in—it had to go up and the oil had to come down.

Mrs. Walker: I don't know which way it came in. It was coming in the minute it hit, to me. When it hit, it seemed like my kitchen, the back windows were going out. When I went out the back door going into my utility room, I had to push. Something had fallen against the door. When I got to the back door, I guess it had been blown out, I had no trouble getting out the back. Something kept on telling me it was the hot water tank—anyhow it was hard to push open. I ran clean to the fence and the smoke followed me. When I got to the back fence I said, "I can't get over it cause of this ol' long gown on so I just went on out to the edge of the fence and got to the edge of the smoke. I can remember standing there hollering when I saw him come out of the black smoke. He was hollering "O Lordy, O Lordy." I went to the next back-door house and got into some clothes and got a coat for myself and a coat for him and he grabbed an old spread off the bed or a comfort off those people's bed. There was no one in there. I grabbed it and threw it around him and stepped in a pair of shoes that was there beside the bed. And then he said "I got to go get the boy out."

Mr. Wesley: May I ask you this question? When you first heard the explosion, did you hear any type of plane noise?

Mrs. Walker: No, I thought it was a car. Just like a car says "putt, putt"—just like it was about to go dead. But it didn't alarm me. It went "putt, putt." You know how Piatt is. It's a busy street. I just heard "putt, putt." Look like it was just a second or so and after I heard that. Just that great thundering . . . just like it just was continuing explosion after explosion. The way it sounded to me.

Mr. Wesley: Were there several explosions?

Mrs. Walker: Yes, it was several. Just like you strike firecrackers—several of them. And the house just looked like rockets.

Mr. Carpenter: Will you go on, Mrs. Walker, and tell us more of your experiences?

Mrs. Walker: Well . . . .

Mr. Wesley: After you got your clothing, where did you receive your first help?

Mrs. Walker: The first girl that tried to get me was the Perry girl—Gertie Mae. What her last name was I don't know. She used to be a Perry. The first one tried to get me to go home with her. She was trying to get me to walk on over to her house. She lived way over on Kansas. About that time his friend . . . .

Mr. Walker: James Nelson.

Mrs. Walker: . . . came up and we going to get you to the hospital. Someone said, "You're cut too; you go on too." And I said, "I hadn't noticed that I was cut." Blood was just streaming down my leg. I didn't even know I was cut. I bled lots more than he did. Cause it cut a vein right down the side of my leg there. We got in there and we couldn't hardly get to the hospital, trucks were coming and they were stopping us. And we had to go almost up to twenty-fourth street. Up to Logopedics[4] . . . across twenty-first . . . .

Mr. Carpenter: Were there any policemen to your knowledge around the area keeping traffic?

Mrs. Walker: Yeah, they were there and they were telling people to get back and everything . . . but they did not come to talk to us.

Mr. Walker: The fellow didn't have a horn, but he told the policemen that he had some victims. And he told us to wait a few minutes because they were going to set some emergency shelter. But I told him we didn't have time to wait on that.

Mr. Carpenter: What hospital did you go to?

Mr. Walker: We went to Wesley.

Mr. Carpenter: How did they treat you over there?

Both: Oh, just wonderful! They were standing waiting on us—waiting on more than us, but I think we were the only two that went to Wesley at that particular time . . . some came in later . . . after that . . . we were the first ones.

Mr. Walker: The biggest part of them went to St. Francis.

Mrs. Walker: They put us both in the same room. For a while until they got to working on him and found out that the tendons on his big toe was cut and they had to work on that so long and they took me out of the room with him and put me in another room.

Mr. Carpenter: I noticed Mr. Walker, you have scars on your forehead. Did you receive those in the . . . ?

Mr. Walker: Yeah, I received those and scars all over my face, back, and I got a rash out of it too.

Mr. Carpenter: Do you still have recurrence of this rash now?

Mr. Walker: Yes, I certainly do.

Mr. Carpenter: What does the doctor say causes this?

Mr. Walker: The doctor says it's nerves; but I don't know. But I can't take a bath.

Mrs. Walker: It's nerves and he breaks out.

Mr. Walker: It look like blood shots run out all over my face, arms and everything. They gave me some medicine to take the sting out of it. But I can't take a bath—just my whole backside turn just as red, between my legs, my foot and everything—just turn just as red. And before he gave me this medicine over here, I just almost be ready to die. At least for a couple hours with it.

Mr. Wesley: This is all during the time you're taking a bath?

Mr. Walker: Yeah, yeah, mostly when I'm taking a bath. I only have this when I take a bath.

Mr. Wesley: When you hear a plane flying over now, how do you feel?

Mr. Walker: Well, it nervouses you.

Mrs. Walker: It appears to me that I want to get out and see which way it's going. I just want to know whether it's coming down or going up. Seem like the house be trembling—lot of times I don't think it is—it's me! Very nervous. I been back to the doctor.

In the course of the interview, Mr. Walker credited the Red Cross with aid in the form of transportation, purchase of glasses and shoes, a food allowance for about four weeks, and a month's rent and utility bills. Operation Holiday, a somewhat informally conducted activity to help needy families at Christmas, aided with a table and some clothing, but proved disappointing in relation to expectations concerning additional articles of furniture. The Walkers also received a total of fifty dollars from two churches in the Negro part of Wichita.

In lieu of prosecuting a claim through Air Force channels, they chose to file a suit against the federal government. A year after the crash, Mr. and Mrs. Walker were described as frustrated and bitter concerning the federal government's discharge of its responsibilities to them resulting from the crash.[5]

The Joseph E. Mason Story

The Reverend Joseph E. Mason, who lives at 1802 North Piatt, was one of the earliest spectators on the scene, arriving there before the first fire engine. He told of his experiences and reactions in the course of an interview conducted in April, 1965.

> Well, I got up first of all that Saturday morning, looking forward to going to Wichita State University game with St. Louis, which was to be in the afternoon at 1:00. Rev. W. G. Williams and I were going because his father pastored in St. Louis. He wanted to see the game. We had no tickets, we had to wait till Saturday morning to get the tickets. The tickets that were left over were sold at 9:00 Saturday morning. So I had gone out there and purchased a couple of tickets for the game and had just returned and was calling him to tell him that I had received the tickets. My folks were getting ready to eat breakfast; they sleep late on Saturday morning anyway. About the time I got on the telephone to call him, I had just connected him and told him that I had tickets for the game and had made a temporary appointment with him to pick him up at 12:30 so that we could be at the game when it started. By the time I got that finished, the explosion took place. We didn't know what it was but it was a loud noise and he said, "What's

going on down there? What are you doing?" I said, "I don't know, somebody probably ran into the car or the house." We've had several wrecks from the car where people ran into the side of the house or up into our yard. I'd better hang up and see what's happening so I hung up and told him I'd pick him up at 12:30. Then I went to the door and looked out and I could see a billow of black smoke just pouring up into the air, it was very intense. I told my son, "Let's go up there quickly." I had my pickup truck parked headed north, I had just come back from Wichita State; so we jumped in it and drove as quickly as we could. As we drove up we could see pieces of the plane alongside the streets.

I got within a half a block of the disaster area—not a half block of where the impact was, but I got to half a block of Nineteenth Street. So I got out and as I got out, I met this woman. This is the west side of the street. She was bringing water out to pour on the fire; there were several patches of fire that was where grass had caught fire around her car. I said, "What's the matter?" She said, "My new car is on fire." I said, "You never will get it put out like that." She had a little pan carrying water out to it. So I helped her put the fire out around her car and on the upholstery, or whatever had happened to it. Then I went on up the street and as I was going up the street I started over to Rev. Barron of the Tabernacle Baptist Church. I thought I would go over there as quickly as possible but the crowd were gathering and the fire department hadn't arrived as yet. He lived in the Allen house on the east side of the street—was the first house at the corner of the impact and his house was second. The houses on the east side of the street were brick and they weren't damaged as much as the ones on the west side of the street. The west side of the street were all in flames. Two houses north of Twentieth Street and then there was several south. It turned out to be five or six I think south of there and they were frame and the JP4 fuel was flowing down the street . . .

could see it. It was green. I worked out at Boeing plant so I recognized it as it was flowing down the street.

People had gathered pretty quickly. There were perhaps . . . they were gathering when I got there, there were some already there. One of the first things that I saw was the man that was crying as he went down the street, just crying 'Oh Lordy, oh Lordy' without anything on but a shirt. It was open and he was a white man and I tried to comfort and asked him what was the matter and he said his boys was in that house. It was Mr. Martin—Joe Martin. That was the house where the boy burned up in front of the house. The boy was in the front—he was burning . . . you could see him burning—and the other we found later had gone to the back door. He had two boys there.

Quite a bit of debris was over the area. You could see the houses that you could see where there were pieces of metal that had hit some of them. The neighbor houses on the corner of . . . we will come back a little farther because Paul Childress' was the second house from Nineteenth Street on the east side of the street and he had an old car setting out in front of this place—an old Chevy and then he had this Cadillac up in his driveway and the old car sitting out in front was headed north and the windshield and the back glass were both broken out by the concussion or something that went through. His Cadillac sitting up in front, he had a '58 Cadillac sitting in the driveway, it had a piece gone through his back glass on the driver's side.

I saw Mr. Martin, but we did not discuss his experiences. His sister-in-law used to live two doors north of here. She was a Mrs. Smith and when we moved up into this area they were living there and they had gone back east and she read in the paper about what had happened and they came to the funeral and she was talking with friends in Valley Center and she called me and she related to me the experience that he had related to her.

That was while she was still here. Before they went to the funeral they went to Arkansas. They took the boys to Arkansas.

After leaving that point and after quieting Mr. Martin enough to at least find out how many boys were in the house, I went on immediately over to Rev. U. W. Barron's because I knew him and I was interested in seeing what had happened there. The house next door wasn't on fire as yet but it was just beginning to catch on fire. The girls were in there and they said they got out but we carried all the stuff out of Rev. Barron's home and out of the basement. All of his furniture, after we found out that the house wasn't on fire but then the next one north was burning so we perhaps thought that this one would catch on fire and in order to keep it—if it did catch on fire from getting water-logged—so we were carrying things out of his house and the third house, we carried everything out of those two houses.

Everything was carried to the alley and back to the fence and several people were there and somebody said that they were beginning to pick it up and some of his members had come and one man had a truck and he said "I will watch it while you bring it out"—everybody had volunteered, you know. In the front bedroom there was a little bank that looked like a safe with some coins, so in order to keep something from happening to it, one of the fellows said "You had better take this out and give it to Deacon out there." One of the deacons was out there with this truck to carry this stuff away, to put in a basement where they had planned to move it, and so I took the bank, of course, it had a little change. Somebody might have taken it so I took it out and Mrs. Barron happened to be out there at that time and I gave it to her.

Pretty soon the police came with the dogs and they ran nearly everybody away. I think while we were still carrying the furniture out the police came. They didn't bother very many of the ones that were working. They ran a number of the people back because they knew there would be looting. Then the firemen came as I was down there talking to Mr. Martin. They were just getting there and I thought, my goodness, it sure took them a long time to get the water. We learned later that the mains were ruptured and they couldn't get water out of them and that was one reason. They had to find some other main that had water that wasn't ruptured so that was one of the reasons for the delay.

After the police ran everybody back we—Rev. Barron was out standing outside of the house and Rev. Martin of St. Paul's Church, he was there and he told the police that we are ministers and the Rev. Barron lives here so he didn't bother us. They just left us alone and they were running so many of the other people back, getting them out of the way and out of the area and getting them back out of the fire, too. I stood there I think until about 11:00 when I came home. I came home around11:00, I believe it was, because I came home to eat and I wouldn't have eaten then, I wouldn't have come then, but my son Keith came up after me. He had already gone back and he said that they were coming from a different radio station and newspaper that they wanted an interview with me. Somebody had gotten my voice on walkie-talkie there and somebody had used me earlier in the disaster.

We had several calls when I came home around 11:00 there were several calls that I was taking that is the reason I came home, because people came after me and Keith and Jan came up to me and said "Daddy, they are calling you from all over the country and we want you to come home." I never did eat breakfast, so I came home and then between calls I was trying to eat breakfast because I wanted to get back up there as quickly as possible. Cleveland called twice, I believe, New York called three times and California two calls and Oklahoma City had called and St. Louis called twice.

I'm a good friend of C. W. Walker. I was with him at a NAACP meeting several Sundays ago and he had just started back to work. He's the man that ran out of

> the house, broke out the window, and went out in his birthday suit. He was getting ready to take a bath when the explosion hit. You know the explosion was directly in front of his house on the northwest corner of Twentieth and Piatt, and he said that any other Saturday they would have been in the front room with their breakfast trays watching TV. That's what they usually do on Saturday morning. But that Saturday morning he guessed the Lord wasn't ready for him. That's the way he put it. He's comical anyway if you know him. He said it was his number and right on his street, but it just wasn't his time.
>
> Walker was—you talk about shook up—he was shook up. He was just incoherent. That night someone went to the hospital and you could hardly understand what he was saying, because of the experience. And it was quite a while before he went back to work. Of course, some of the employers have insurance that cover you while you're off. I believe they call it payroll insurance. It pays a small wage while you're off and takes care of your expenses: your hospitalization and doctor's bill.

Asked whether the disaster had affected his beliefs in connection with the daily life that he leads, he responded.

> No, the only thing I thought—we ministers changed our subject for the Sunday sermon. . . . My Sunday sermon was, "You'd better get ready—it comes like a thief in the night." It was a judgment for some people and there's no doubt about it.
>
> We gave the basketball tickets to Rev. Williams and Alfred Moore. These are the deacon's sons. I didn't feel like going. I called him and said I didn't feel like going to the game and he didn't feel like it either. I wanted to go back up there, and so I called the boys and Mrs. Williams took them to the game.

Captain Richards' Story

Captain Artie A. Richards, Jr., of the fire department, lives at 2106 North Minnesota, just 200 feet west of the crash. He was sitting in his front room waiting to take his wife to the doctor, Saturday morning, when, at about 9:30,

> I heard engines making a lot of noise and they sounded like they were right over the house. So, I went to get up to see what was causing the noise and about that time I was knocked to the floor. I got up off the floor, looked through the back window, and the air was full of exploding parts from the airplane. I realized then that there had been a crash and just about that same instant, it exploded and when it exploded, there was a wall of flames approximately 300 feet high and I would say about a block long. At that same time, there was a lot of panic. People were screaming, running, and immediately I thought of evacuating the people on the block. So I got my wife out and then I started walking door to door, beating on the doors, telling the people to evacuate and go to Twenty-First and Minnesota.
>
> After I had got people evacuated from that block, I tried to call in a fire alarm. The fire alarm phone was busy. So then, I came on back down the block opening gates, letting pets out, as they were terrified too. And then I went around the corner. When I got to the corner of Twentieth and Minnesota, I saw Mrs. Walker. She was in a state of shock. . . . the plane hit right in front of her house; in fact, we got two bodies out of her front bedroom. One of the crew members of the aircraft, and her roomer were in the front bedroom, and he actually never knew what happened.
>
> I actually didn't do too much fire fighting because I was helping in the rescue part of it.

Captain Richards confirms that by the time the top fire and police officials reached the scene, whatever initial hysteria there had been had subsided into a kind of dull shock. He sent no one to the hospital but concentrated instead upon evacuating the living. Looking at the conflagration, he wrote off the entire west side of the 19th and 20th blocks on North Piatt. "That was a terrifying experience, too. It was fifteen degrees outside that morning, if you remember, and I was in my shirtsleeves and I was plenty warm."

Chief Simpson assigned Richards to help the inspection department try to establish names and addresses of the houses which had burned. This was done largely with the help of the mailman for that route, who happened to come through at the time. He spent a half-hour or so with the firemen, attempting to associate names and addresses with the burned houses and to establish the number of persons residing in each. They also called upon surrounding neighbors for help. This task completed, Richards proceeded to help with the tagging and removal of bodies. He was released from duty at about 4:00 P.M.

"How did it feel, going back into your house and thinking of what lay immediately behind it?"

"The one thought was just how lucky we were because just one-hundred feet more to the east could just as well been us as those people on Piatt—could have been Minnesota. We were just lucky. It's a pretty sobering thought."

He and his wife sat at their back window that night and watched as Air Force personnel, working under floodlights, collected debris. Richards went back on duty at 8:00 A.M. on the 17th.

The James Garmon Story

James Garmon operated a sundry store at 1901 East Twenty-First at the time of the crash. It was located between Minneapolis and Minnesota in a complex of units, one of which was to become emergency headquarters for the Air Force and relief agencies. On the 16th he opened his store at about 9:00 in the morning. "The milkman had just brought the milk in and I was putting the milk away and I heard a plane that was real low and I made a remark to the milkman, 'That plane is awfully low.' Then about that time we heard a blast and he and I both looked outside and people were running, so we went outside also. I got around to the alley about the time the plane crashed. There was definitely an explosion before the plane crashed."

Asked to reiterate that comment, he continued: "Before it crashed. This explosion shattered the windows at the other end of this building—down where the Air Force set up their emergency offices."

This pre-crash explosion, in Garmon's estimation, broke the display windows at Razook's supermarket, located on 21st Street, just east of Piatt and adjacent to the field which the plane barely missed.

> Then, I immediately came back and went and tried to lock my door and I couldn't lock it. I broke the key off in the door in fact, so I just left the doors open and I ran down to the crash scene. All you could do was stand there. I never felt so helpless in my life because there was just a wall of smoke and flame as high as you could see. You could not enter. All you could do was just stand there and be helpless, and there was people coming in their housecoats and whatever they could have on at that particular time, coming out. We directed a lot of them to come in out of the cold, because it was quite chilly that morning—to come into the store and take refuge.
>
> The little boy whose jacket burned and stuck to his back—the Jackson boy—he passed me going to the filling station and I never noticed it until later and you could hear the sound like of ammunition going off, which could have been accumulators [pressure accumulators for activating the hydraulic system] or anything like that on the plane going off in the area.

Returning to the store, Mr. Garmon found fewer people there than he had expected. This was a phenomenon of the local citizen reaction: those affected by the crash who were neither hospitalized nor killed had been taken in by neighbors, friends, and relatives. This, incidentally, later caused some difficulty in establishing lists of survivors, injured, and deceased. Garmon did not turn in an alarm—it had probably seemed a superfluous act—but by the time he returned to the store, he heard the equipment coming. "It seemed as though the fire-fighting equipment would never get here, but it did. It got here as fast as possible."

The store at the eastern end of the elongated U-shaped building in which Garmon's business was located was empty, and the

Negro businessman called the landlord, Byron Smith, to get the key and permission to use it for emergency purposes.

Like others, he saw little hysteria. "Everybody was pretty calm. There was a little hysteria . . . some of the ladies and smaller children were crying and asking questions about other people that they was concerned about, you see." But the overwhelming response was a mixture of surprise and shock.

Garmon's recollection is that the Air Force set up its emergency claims office in mid-afternoon—"I would say about 3:00, may have been earlier or it may have been later. They had it set up pretty well." Some 60 per cent of the affected persons in the neighborhood were his customers, and because of his familiarity with them and the Air Force personnel's familiarity with him, it was natural that he be given access to the claims office and asked to help. "The first thing we did . . . we went to locate the next-of-kin to the ones that they found out was actually dead and locate their next kin so that we could notify them so that a definite executor would be appointed to know who to make these claims.

"We went to the mortuaries and found out who was dead, then we took the directories and everything to try to find them. Phone books and everything to try to find out the next-of-kin. Then we called different people to refer you to someone else who is out of town and things of this sort and locate them that way."

This took place after the bodies had been identified at the morgue and sent to mortuaries, according to Garmon. He was aided in this effort by Edwin Sexton, Jr., a local publisher, and politician of sorts, who had served a nominal appointive term as state senator. "The courthouse was opened up and I had access to the records. The next thing we did after we located the next-of-kin was to locate the property owners. This was done through the courthouse to locate the property owner and also this served a dual purpose to establish the value of the land and the value of the improvement on the land and help make a final adjustment on the property that was completely destroyed or some part of it was destroyed."

Garmon was included in an *ad hoc* committee set up by the Red Cross. Composed of a cross-section of local businessmen and professional men, the committee, which met periodically at the combined Red Cross-Air Force emergency headquarters in Byron Smith's building to hear complaints about the conduct of the emergency operation, reports from the Red Cross director and Air Force claims officer, and, generally, to give an air of community oversight to the operation.

Mr. Garmon, a man of entrepreneurial instinct, proved quite understanding of and sympathetic with the problems and efforts of the Red Cross and the Air Force. Whereas Rev. Reynolds stressed the communications gap and misunderstanding, the timidity of uneducated Negroes in dealing with professionals, filling out interminable forms, and proving ownership, Jim Garmon philosophizes:

> There will always be misunderstanding and rumors such as the thousand dollars available, just come up and ask for it, instead of people finding out the real truth and, in fact, this is what Sexton and my position was, to contact these people and tell them exactly where they stood and to explain the things to them. But we did have difficulty with the attorneys on this, because the attorneys and the ministers were instructing them never to sign any papers whatsoever. But the way the Air Force has it, it was just as plain as day that you could not be cheated. This was available to them, they could read it themselves, and it was not a final settlement, but the Air Force could not start working on a claim until they signed a paper that they do have a claim, so this was one thing that delayed a lot of these things being settled, because you couldn't get the people to sign a claim.

Garmon feels that he acted as go-between for victims and relief agencies, in helping to secure needed funds for eligible persons and attempting to persuade victims that rather than to inflate their temporary claims, it would be better to request only enough to meet present needs and later to maximize the ultimate payment on the claim.

He thought the efforts of the Ministerial League (discussed in Chapter 7), were well-intended but ill-directed: "Yes, the ministerial league all met and they was going to try to raise funds for the disaster groups. This was real fine, and to get clothing and things of this sort for them. But they ran into a problem. They get these things but they do not know how to disperse and who needs it and who doesn't. It is always better if they would channel this stuff to the Red Cross."

The Richard Jackson Story

Richard Jackson, who resides at 1546 North Piatt, told his story to interviewers Leonard Wesley and Frank Carpenter on May 5, 1965.

> The morning of the crash I was in bed at the time and I heard the plane in the background and all of a sudden there was a tremendous explosion and I completely flipped in the bed. I immediately jumped out of the bed and looked out of the window into the back yard and there wasn't any destruction of any kind there. I immediately looked out the front window. And directly there was a B-52 type aircraft flying in front of my house at not too high altitude. I immediately recognized the plane as a B-52 aircraft of Boeing. It also happens that my father is a flight-test engineer.
>
> I put on my pants and ran out the door and looked up the street and there was pillars of smoke and flame up the street and I returned to the house and explained to my wife that there had been an air crash and slipped into my shoes and started running up the street. Ten minutes after the crash, approximately, I was in the area. The first thing I did about two and a half blocks from the actual crash was to pick a part of the aircraft. So many people were pouring out of the houses that these bits and parts were beginning to be kicked around and picked over. I picked a part to identify it as either an Air Force plane or a Boeing plane or a commercial plane. Having picked up this part that I was unable to identify, and that I was a Boeing engineer for seven years, I thought possibly that I might identify the part. I picked up a part and carried it about a block away and put it among other parts that had been gathered there. I immediately continued into the crash area.

The streets were burning, the automobiles that were parked on the street were burning and I chased a group of people from around a burning truck in hopes that the gasoline would not explode and I continued into the intersection all the way into the actual crater itself. At that point I was looking for a friend of mine, a Mr. Harvey Love, who lives on the corner of the intersection of the actual crash. His house had completely disappeared. In milling around the house I was unable to find out if anyone had got out of the house. In the meantime, the house on the southeast corner was burning and Rev. Barron lives next door to that house and I immediately ran into that house and started carrying articles out and put them over the fence in the neighbor's yard for protection.

After doing this, I bumped head-on into Harvey Love as he was returning home from work from the packing company and I was the first one he talked to and he asked me if I had seen his family. At that time I asked him if his family was preparing to leave the house when he went to work. He said, "No." He had left them in bed. And I said that I had checked the neighborhood and asked around to different people if anyone had seen them. I'm awful afraid that they did not get out of the crash. At that time I continued to look around the area trying to identify the parts of plane that I did know. At that time I didn't know whether two planes had collided or what had happened. There was so little left of the plane that I was unable to identify the plane even though I was familiar with Boeing procedures, part numbers, etc.

Completing the survey, the fire trucks, the Air Force personnel had begun to arrive and people were asked to relocate from the immediate area and I among them saw that I could be of no further help, went home to explain to my wife exactly what had happened.

Due to the people hearing the crash scene, hearing the noise, they just kind of stopped right there. Fire trucks were unable to get through and ambulances

> were unable to get through. And they seemed to stop just where they were, and blocking all exits and entrances into the area. The police department had their loudspeakers out asking people to move, asking people to stand away from the fire and the area so they could put out the fire. The streets were still burning and some buildings were burning and of course vehicles that were parked on the street were. There was a body laying in the front yard of one of the buildings. It seems that the individual, that I was unable to identify, started out of the building and got as far as the front door and fell dead as he entered into the yard. There was rubble and water over ankle deep in the area, fuel floating and burning as it ran into lower level. But as far as anyone being in charge, no, I don't think any one person was in charge at that particular time because I think the people who were there to help were still in the state of shock. The different people who attempted to take authority—their main interest was to get people away from the houses, away from the area in case there were other explosions which might take place and injure more people.

This is how the crash affected some of those who lived long enough to understand the nature of the disruption which had occurred in their lives. (See Appendix A for fatalities.) Just as the nature of the injury incurred, if any, varies greatly, so the reactions range widely on the spectrum of human emotions. What all shared was the momentary sense of shock—of stupefaction—which would undoubtedly be the initial response of any similarly affected group, no matter how different their composition. Almost as common as the initial shock, and of immensely greater importance in terms of the psychology of response to the disaster, was the quickness with which apathy born of shock was transformed into a kind of recuperative urge. Neighborhood residents acted singly and in groups toward improving chances for survival and minimizing physical harm and material damage. They reacted even before they could gauge the magnitude and precise agent of the explosive fireball which threatened or extinguished them.

VII

A Negro Disaster

Wichita is the largest city in Kansas (population 279,122) and the county seat of Sedgwick County. Located in south-central Kansas, 161 miles southwest of the nation's geographic center, it was established as a town in 1868 and incorporated in 1870. Two years later it had a population of 2,000. The first Negro family arrived in Wichita in 1870. In 1880 the town numbered four Negro families; by 1900, there were some 1,389 Negroes within the city limits—5.6 per cent of the population. According to the 1960 census figures, the Wichita Negro population was 19,681, or 7.8 per cent of the total Wichita population, an increase of 146 per cent over 1950 when there were only 8,082 Negroes in the city. The Negro population rose to an estimated 22,000 in 1963 and "at least" 25,000 in 1965.

Although the process of segregation of housing and schools in Wichita has not yet been subjected to historical study, it is clearly a development of this century. Donald O. Cowgill, Wichita State University sociologist, is quoted in a recent newspaper article:

> As Wichita grew, Cowgill said, it had no racial guidelines, "No one knew what the rules were, so to speak."
>
> "The result," he said, "is that the whites decided to play it safe and segregate everything. Since no one had challenged such segregation before, it remained the state of things.

> "But since that time, Negroes have found that when you do challenge them, the old segregation policies are pretty fragile—except in the case of housing."[1]

An earlier story in the series, from which the sociologist's statement is taken, dealt with education:

> Wichita is a city of racially segregated schools.
>
> The majority of its Negro children never sit in a classroom with white youngsters until high school.
>
> Bleak statistics surround these children. Test scores show them lagging far behind the citywide academic average. Their ability to read is about two grade levels below what it should be.
>
> Few ever catch up. Of every four Negro students who enter Wichita's elementary schools, three will not graduate from high school.[2]

The *Wichita Beacon* series provides convincing evidence of the existence in the city, and its tolerance by the majority population, of invidious distinctions based upon race. Collectively, this pattern defines a segregated community, contained, compressed, and repressed within the majority community, lacking adequate communications with public and private decision-makers, and seething with hostility born of poverty, disease, ignorance, and neglect.

While the newspaper series presented the picture of segregation to a wide audience, the story has long been available to those acquainted with a number of reputable studies on the Negro in Wichita.[3] Cowgill and associates are authorities on housing segregation in the city:

> Within the city, the Negro population is very tightly segregated. Ninety per cent of them live in the main Negro district which falls within Tracts 5, 6, 7, 8, 11 and 18. These tracts contain nearly 18,000 Negroes, and . . . Negroes make up nearly all of the population of Tracts 5, 6, and 12. . . . The major change since 1950 has been an expansion of the main Negro district to the east. . . . Wichita is one of the most tightly segregated cities in the nation in terms of residence. In 1950, it was

fourteenth from the top among 211 cities. The growth of the Negro population since then has forced an expansion of the district, but this has not lessened the degree of segregation. On the contrary, its segregation index increased from 91.5 to 95.3 (complete segregation —100).[4]

The Wichita Community Planning Council prepared *A Profile of Wichita* in December 1965, which shows the intensity of various demographic characteristics by census housing tracts. Housing Tract No. 7, in which the crash occurred, is one of the four in Wichita having the largest number of children nineteen years old or younger. Eight (or one-third) of the civilians killed in the disaster were under nineteen, ranging in age from nine months to seventeen years (if we do not count an unborn fetus). Tract No. 7 is also among the three with the highest incidence of Negro population in the city;[5] all but two of the civilians killed were Negroes. It ranks fourth in the total number of welfare cases and falls into the highest category for men and women employed in menial occupations. Although only 26.2 per cent of persons twenty-five-years-old and over have had less than an eighth-grade education (the Wichita average is 27.1 per cent), it is one of the tracts with the largest number of school drop-outs. It is, for the most part, a neat and well cared for area; it ranks in the lowest category of tracts characterized by dilapidated housing. At the same time, it is in the first rank of tracts with overcrowded houses (housing units with more than one person per room). This congestion is reflected in the disaster figures: Five persons of four different surnames were killed at 2037 N. Piatt, five with two different surnames were killed at 2041, and five with three different surnames at 2053. The typically high incidence of one-parent families associated with Negroes prevails in Tract 7.

The disaster affected, and help was proffered to, a relatively concentrated population grouping not in the main stream of American life. Problems, especially in communication and interpretation of motives, inevitably occurred. Some Negroes who witnessed the post-impact relief effort, exaggerated the white-man versus black-man aspect of the operation, and overstated the Negro victims' unfamiliarity with questions, forms, and documentation.

Housing segregation has relevance to the crash and its aftermath in three ways. First, the malicious myth that the KC-135 crew chose their point of impact, preferring to take Negro rather than white lives, does exist in some circles. In the minds of some people, this belief is reinforced by the undeniable fact of housing segregation.[6] The crucial insight here, however, is that dominant community mores, reinforced by such factors as economic status and education levels, produce housing areas in Wichita that are predominantly Negro or predominantly white. Therefore, a crash of this magnitude within the city would be a Negro disaster or a white disaster.

Secondly, the Negro community sees the Red Cross, the Air Force, the police department, the fire department (to a lesser extent), and officialdom in general as White, with a capital "W," and therefore suspect. While this attitude did not appear in the hour of crisis when all pitched in to help, it did emerge in the days of recovery and rehabilitation which followed. The significance of this perception is not sapped by challenges to its accuracy. The persons affected by the crash were suspicious, apprehensive, aloof ("we can take care of ourselves"), or otherwise distant in their relations to the official and quasi-official sources of help. This was not significantly relieved by the presence of Negro airmen in various noncom ratings at the Air Force aid headquarters.

Housing segregation is significant to the crash in yet a third sense. The police and firemen had no time to consider fine points of social mores and worked as a matter of course in cooperation with civilians (mainly Negroes) to control the disaster. However, the civilian and military aid units which came in to help both before and after the fire had been extinguished were at a disadvantage in that they had had little previous contact with the Negro community of Wichita. They were unaware of the intimidating impact of their official forms, professional ways, and persistent interrogation upon a group which was primarily of low education and socio-economic status, and which was also black and suspicious of whites.

Negro "leadership" groups such as the Ministerial League had a vital opportunity to provide liaison between the professionals and the victims. That they succeeded is doubtful, however, for there is ample reason to believe that they mobilized out of a sense of need to protect what "leadership" they possessed rather than to facilitate communication between relief workers and victims.

It is convenient to refer to "the Negro community" rather than to employ the perjorative "ghetto" or the vague designation "northeast." Obviously there are many Negro communities in Wichita, and among Negroes many variant perceptions of the Negro community and of the equally complex white community.

Personal experiences with predominantly white "do-good" groups in Wichita and with others who have a different stereotype of the Negro (garbage on the front lawn, rusting cars in the backyard, ill-cared-for houses) suggest to the author that both the self-styled "good" people among the white population and those who would probably style themselves "realists" and men of "practicality" rest many of their perceptions of and reactions to the Negroes in Wichita on the erroneous premise of a homogeneous Negro community. There is The Negro.

To the contrary, there are variations in aspiration, ability, and socio-economic status, not to mention leadership competition among Negroes who are compelled by circumstances to live in close proximity with each other because of color. These variations will influence people's reactions in a catastrophe. On this last score it is particularly significant to note the fire and police comment upon the (good) behavior of the predominantly Negro crowds in the area, the lack of looting, the communal effort (witnessed by the author at first hand) to empty burning houses of salvable furnishings, the initial dependence of the fire department upon Negro civilians to man hoses, the initial traffic direction undertaken by residents of the neighborhood. Certainly many of the persons, especially the young persons, who engaged in these constructive activities, or at the very worst stood passively by, under other circumstances might have been congregating at street corners and, for lack of other outlets of energy, behaving in a manner likely to court police attention.

By way of final comment on notions of the homogeneity of the "Negro community," it may be noted that the "business community" in the northeast is predominantly white. Twenty-first Street is the dividing line between an *almost* 100 per cent Negro residency area, and a somewhat mixed neighborhood to the north. But "almost," as indicated by the italics, is an important qualification. Upon leaving Mr. Garmon's sundry store, after interviewing him on April 9, 1965, the author encountered Mr. Joe T. Martin, who had resided at 2031 North Piatt, a white man whose two sons were killed in the disaster. He had just returned from Arkansas where he and his wife had buried their two sons. The Martins were unwilling to discuss the crash and its impact upon them. The Martin family was one of the last white families in the vicinity south of 21st Street.

The *Beacon* series on "The Negro in Wichita" identifies two groups of Negro leaders "bound by a common goal but estranged by divergent approaches."[7] These are the moderates and the militants. Although the duality is a gross oversimplification in speaking of leadership in the Negro community in Wichita, as distinguished from Negro civil rights leadership, it did suit the emphasis of the series.

Ample documentation exists that leadership in Negro communities is fully as pluralistic and non-pyramidal, as situational and dependent upon issues and interests, as is leadership in the community at large. Certainly there was no immediate response to the crash which enables one to distinguish the "moderates" from the "militants." Civil rights leadership, like other leadership elements in the community, became evident in the days following the crash, but little or no effort was made by persons identified as civil rights leaders to exploit the incident to that purpose.

Three stages of Negro leadership assertion can be identified in connection with the crash. First, in the hour or two immediately following the crash, persons ranging from the relatively anonymous to those with employment status suggesting latent leadership roles extemporized varying kinds of leadership in varying circumstances. We have referred to the forming of work crews and the augmenting of fire-fighting crews. Ministers, teachers, off-duty city officials, and businessmen helped canalize behavior. In at least one instance, a leadership role, extemporized because of a businessman's proximity to the disaster, was maintained in the days following the crash and ultimately resulted in appointment to the board of directors of the Red Cross.

Secondly, persons of stable leadership status in the Negro community who hardly fit the *Beacon's* dichotomy sought prominent roles for themselves and their organizations in the community response to the crash. This was characteristic, for example, of the Ministerial League. Such individuals and groups formed transient alliances with civil rights leaders to serve their purposes.

Finally, the moderates and the militants found common ground in efforts to succor those affected by the disaster but lost none of their dedication to civil rights. They sought to protect their constituents from victimization by white officialdom, but they also publicly discounted some of the wilder rumors concerning the causes of the crash. These functions were usually consistent with the professional interests of the leaders.

A Negro attorney, speaking with considerable reserve, told interviewers that in racial terms, there was a "nominal reaction" to the crash on the part of Negroes in the community. "Even the Air Force officials were perhaps afraid that since it did happen basically in a Negro community it might arouse racial antagonism toward the Air Force which would be a white instrumentality. There were rumbles on it." By his calculation, normal McConnell flight patterns did not carry Air Force traffic over the Negro part of the city and he would "imagine that you would get many complaints" from other parts of the city within the flight pattern. "In fact, I was out to dinner with a friend of mine who lives in the flight pattern and he was complaining that when the wind was out of the northeast you could hear the house rumble—of course, he said, and I think it is probably true—you get used to something. You hear and you don't hear it. In fact, airplanes are so common around here that you don't look up to watch one. I know I don't; I go about my business."

However, he had heard a number of complaints about the conduct of the investigation and the failure to reveal the cause of the crash:

> Well, there have been a number of complaints. I particularly personally handled complaints. It's been right at three months ago, January 16th and many people want to know what caused the crash. Naturally, if you receive a causation, then one can suggest remedies. If they are overloaded, we can demand that they don't load them so heavily. If the personnel isn't experienced, we can demand that they receive more training or the runway was too short or for any reason. . . . And many of the heirs of the deceased want to know what the cause was and I'm not sure the Air Force is going to disclose it. But I do know that they have these crack teams, they are about as expert and technical as any teams come and I would think by now that they would be able to render a report as to the cause. And I do know that the initial statement about the pilot attempting to land on this field . . . nobody believes this hogwash! Because you can't put a KC-135 tanker in a two-by-four field . . . with it out of control too—it just can't be done . . . . That's like landing in a basketball court on the moon. Anyhow, this was said and I think this was an emotional reaction from the Air Force. Many people want to know what caused it. It's like an automobile accident . . . you want to know where the fault lies. Who is the one who precipitated it. And knowing air crashes, something caused it; it didn't just happen.

Inevitably, communications difficulties resulted from the crash. Mass media stories could be interpreted by listeners or readers of a certain level of sophistication as an invitation to all those remotely or directly affected by the crash to go to the temporary Air Force headquarters on 21st Street near Minnesota and collect $1,000 cash. Resentment arose when such persons learned at the headquarters that documentation of relationships, property ownership, and damage was necessary. Despite a significant sprinkling of Negro Air Force personnel in the claims office, many applicants felt that these requirements reneged on promises publicly made and challenged their honesty. Great suspicion and concern emerged, in many instances, when applicants were required to sign documents which, to the best of their knowledge, might constitute a waiver of claim or an indication of satisfaction with a less-than-adequate claim.

The attorney referred to above did not feel that such complaints were warranted, understandable as they might be:

> You couldn't ask for anything more. A person comes up and says that my house was damaged. They have a right to ask that you show title to the property—to a person whose house is damaged, the roof is off, he thinks it is going to rain on him, he can probably be chagrined—immediate relief was not forthcoming—of course, they have got to follow Air Force regulations—I found considerable sympathy on behalf of Air Force officials showed their willingness to do anything that they could do within their power—even in terms of paying subsidies to relatives who would come in and in some instances not even being sure of the legality of some of them. They took the person's word for it and took the position that the people were telling the truth until it was proven differently, as opposed to taking a position that you're telling a damn lie and when we find you are not lying we'll do something then. . . .
>
> Of course the Air Force in this instance had a relatively easy job. Because the tragedy was such that the people were either wiped out or else they were not hurt too badly. A death matter is a lot easier to handle than an injury matter. Or say some person who was a block away from the crash had a heart attack. Now did he have this heart attack because the time had come in his life he would have had the damn thing if the plane had not crashed or was the crash a factor—these are just some very touch-and-go precipitating questions. But, if they had a bunch of injuries, fifty or sixty injuries, they would have had a tremendous problem on their hands.

He was not so tolerant of the efforts of other groups, including the Red Cross:

> The Red Cross, naturally, is an agency which collects thousands of dollars a year on a very logical appeal

> to a person's emotions, sense of decency, and sense of wanting to help someone else and in many instances those things that they announce as practices never come up to their announcements. There were some housing instances—the home builders and others again made these wild promises about making housing available. These things are done more to help the local group who makes them than to help the beneficiaries. I don't see this as discrimination, but as an effort by these private agencies to get in opportunism, to get a feather in their cap. Plus there was a discriminatory factor. Wichita is a rigidly Jim Crow housing city or there would be many people who would volunteer housing. And as you know that the housing that was available was run down, shabby, shot, uninhabitable for the most part.

Insurance adjusters and the insurance companies, generally, came under the attorney's experienced and baleful scrutiny. In this instance, he thought they had not performed too badly, but for a special reason—they knew they would not be left holding the bag: "I deal with, I don't know how many insurance companies—I've dealt with insurance companies perhaps for years—I find most of them to be very conservative and unfair." Asked what he meant by "conservative," he said:

> Not willing to pay the just cost, the just price. You know they are willing to take your premiums, but when the time comes to pay off they want to either over-depreciate or pay you less than your claim is worth or try to make you over-substantiate your claim, where in fact you can't do it. In this instance, I found the insurance companies to be very fair, not because they had a sudden change of heart, but knowing they were subrogated, which means legally that they would be paid back by the Air Force. They didn't press the point. If you pressed them, they would say, "We'll pay it." Because they are not going to lose on it. If it were not for the subrogation aspect, I would imagine that we would be hasseling all over the place, trying to get a settlement on some of these things.

Concerning cases where the insurance agency said that claimed damages were not so severe and refused to pay, he explained:

> Yes, there are some instances where this has happened. Some people who were near the crash site, put in claims for damage and I am investigating one now. This was an exception rather than the rule. The Air Force officials themselves were surprised. This goes back to innate prejudice, and something you can't really prove, but it lies dormant in our society, a feeling by the majority of white people that Negroes are innately inferior, they won't say this publicly, but they believe it. Their actions prove it. And you can tell this by the officers and the non-com personnel at the crash site or the station. They just knew that they would be deluged with complaints from all over the place. They were really shocked. In fact they had to go look up the complainants in most instances, particularly on relocation because the average disasteree would rather live with the relatives, particularly in his emotional state, than to go to some vacant house. There is excitement and psychologically, people having been through this want to talk about it and this makes them the central figure of the hour. This is a factor too, that arises. They [Air Force personnel] were sitting back knowing that they would be just overcome with all of "these false claims" and with people trying to take advantage of the government. Well, this didn't happen. And I told them that it wouldn't happen. But they soon learned that it didn't.

Asked about the conduct of city officials and employees, including police, at the site of the crash, he voiced a set of perceptions, particularly concerning the police, which varies from that of police officials. (It is not the *fact* of the matter which is important, but the stereotypical perception. Whether it is possible to guard against such perceptions, and how best to do so, are matters to which the present inquiry cannot be directed.)

> We understand that several of the city agencies had met to try to map out plans as to what they would do in the

event of a tragedy of this kind or some other kind. Are you aware of this meeting?

"No, I'm not. I have no knowledge of any committee of this kind."

How do you think Wichita actually responded in terms of the fire department, the police with their cooperation or lack of it with the air base personnel? How do you think this community action was mobilized?

"I think—there again—it is difficult for me to be completely accurate. In order to be accurate, I would have to have some comparative basis on which to make a conclusion. I would say that from what I was able to observe, they did all they could do. There were some complaints about these police dogs. The crowds, in all fairness to the police department, the crowds were interfering with the normal progress of cleaning up the area and they did have the dogs out. Of course, Negroes hate dogs. Everybody hates dogs. They make you feel like an animal, snapping at your heels, barking at you—people were scared to death—you're scared of them anyhow, see. There were some complaints on that and of course the officers threatened to call the paddy wagon—they never did. Whereas in some instances they probably could have done so and got away with it legally, but I guess they figured the place was in enough emotional upheaval without stirring up the place anymore, you see."

We heard some of the radio announcers say that people would be arrested if they arrived on the scene. We later found out that this was initiated by the radio stations. Is this true or is it a rumor?

"Some of the police officials were threatening arrest if the people didn't move back, if they didn't move on, if they blocked the streets, if they didn't get out of the way of the firemen and the Air Force investigators. But I can see there is a reasonable basis for this. Nobody was in fact arrested for this—I know. And the threat of it sometimes has the same weight as the actual fact itself."

Dogs have, of course, become a symbol to the Negro, when employed by police. The United States Commission on Civil Rights, for example, in its Mississippi Report of April, 1964, referred to "citizens of the United States" having been "set upon by vicious dogs, beaten and otherwise terrorized because they sought to vote." The question of the viciousness of police-controlled dogs is not relevant to a consideration of the image which Negroes entertain of dogs whose leashes are in the hands of police. Informal checking with a high police official reveals that one police dog was employed effectively at a point where crowds were trampling on airplane debris which was deemed essential to the analysis of causes of the crash. According to this police view the dog was employed in the same manner and toward the same purpose as dogs that have been used on other occasions—to clear sidewalks opposite high schools in town, to mention but a single example.

We have, of course, reached a point in the United States where acts which decades ago would have had no noticeable racial implications are now fraught with such overtones. To what extent law enforcement and other government activities should be guided by the effort to avoid symbols which are anathema to Negroes is a question recognized as germane but left unanswered in this study.

If the Negro attorney was conservative in his reaction to the Negro overtones of the disaster, a Negro minister, recently moved to the community, was less so. At the time of the disaster and interview he was the president of the Ministerial League, a predominently Negro ministerial group. Educated at Philander Smith College in Little Rock, he had also done work at Eden Theological Seminary and the University of Nebraska. At the moment of the crash, he was taking an examination for a class which he attended at Wichita State University, whose field house was narrowly missed by the plane as it arched toward the crash. His church was located in what he described as "a Negro community"—in part by choice and in part "by the unwritten law."

I say by choice; I think this needs to be qualified because I am reminded what conditioning does. I don't want to go into detail. But you can't tell this family that you can't buy a house for four generations and expect that the fifth generation, who's in exactly the same will change as far as far as wanting to go out immediately and buy a house. They have been conditioned to this kind of thing. This is one reason why it is difficult and one of the biggest concerns across the country now. The impetus is coming out of the college students. This is because their minds have been stimulated. The youngster who doesn't go to college, he's contented to dig the ditch and to live in what we call the ghetto. The one that goes to college wants better because his mind has been elevated. This conditioning, as long as the man is uneducated will continue on the present level. This is what is referred to as the ghetto; people don't like it—the area going up to Twenty-first and across. Now, of course, everyone wants to move across Twenty-first Street. Psychologically why—because it means moving out of the ghetto. Even those who are in it don't like it. And this evidence of moving across Twenty-first Street—if it appears they are going to open up across Mead, then it will be across Mead; if it opens up across Central, then it will be Central because it is the idea of getting out. Though we're not going to demonstrate or raise a lot of noise about the right to do it. We were not conditioned this much but as soon as someone opens the door we'll respond. Most of them I think would say are not anxious to move out on Broadview. They're anxious to move out; it's the idea that I want to move out of this area of where I've been labeled as being a low class citizen.

I was having a final examination at Wichita State University and my mind was crowded with trying to remember what the author said about Jody who is a lad who has some problems and other writers and characters in the area of juvenile delinquency, the class which I was taking. The plane came over—the class noticed how low

> it was and made comment about this and wondered what it was and shortly after this, we had the break and we could see the smoke—we thought that something has happened, but we were certainly hoping that not a plane had gone down, but maybe what we saw was actually excess gas from the refinery. I left class at 11:30, I was picked up by my wife who reported to me at that time that the airplane had gone down and it had gone down near a member of our church, Mrs. Fred Balenton who lives at 2127 Piatt.

Finding that his parishioner was safe, the minister returned his family to their home and began to function in his role as president of the League.

> I then got on the phone and as a president of the Ministerial League, began trying to contact the ministers being certain that many people of the churches would be affected by this and they would need help. Secondly, was there an organization within the community that would make itself available to the community in whatever ways of service that we could be. I didn't know what areas of service this would be but I thought this was something that needed to be done. We knew the Red Cross and Air Force would be there, but by mid-afternoon many things were happening. Many things were being sent and by five or six o'clock that evening I was more convinced than before that there needed to be an organization trying to work within the community and assimilating information and right kinds of information so that evening the Ministerial League had met.

It is difficult to evaluate this conviction that a local group should be activated. Undoubtedly it was a reflection—warranted or not—of Negro sense of need for a Negro relief organization in contradistinction to the Red Cross, Air Force, and city officialdom, who were perceived as essentially white and, to a degree, alien to the community. Yet if this sense of insularity guided the Negro leaders' response to the disaster, their feelings were sufficiently ambivalent that they simultaneously counseled reliance upon the "white" relief agencies.

Now there was Mrs. Craven. After I counseled her regarding the desire of Air Force and Red Cross to help those persons affected by it, reverse her initial position and go to them. I did counsel with her. She was very pleased that this information was there. She went to the Red Cross. The Red Cross said "yes," they would take care of her so that her hospital bill regarding this was taken care of. What else was taken care, I don't know. One of the things that took place as an example, you remember the mass media carried that there is $1,000 available for families involved in the disaster. Such poor publicity should never be released. I was opposed to the statement, many that I found was not true. At that time the statement was made the actual fact of the matter is that there is $250 available from the Air Force. The Red Cross had any money available but they were meeting emergencies as always. It wasn't dependent upon the disaster. Red Cross or whatever you see, there is a disaster of any nature the Red Cross stands ready to serve.

By mid-afternoon there was already on the news media that one of the television stations was setting up a disaster fund to be channeled through the Fourth National Bank to be administered by the Red Cross. It was immediately placed that the Red Cross would be available to meet their need. The Red Cross and Air Force are the main two. This isn't to take away from the Salvation Army's doing, but it was Red Cross who sent out word that we need gas, we need heaters of some kind. So here, this is not an oversight of the work of the Salvation Army, but rather that these other two became foremost in our minds so that the not-mentioning of them is on this account.

Negro participation was organized by those persons in the community with a vested interest in making themselves visible under such circumstances—the Negro preachers, whose position within the Negro community, with respect to the retention of segregated Negro neighborhoods, and institutions, was ambivalent. This is not to say that the Ministerial League was single-purposed or mendacious in the action which it took in response to their president's leadership. Other *ad hoc* efforts were also developing around town, some self-serving (all one had to do was to offer help to gain free newspaper and radio advertising), some altruistic; some pinpointed to specific and real needs, some diffuse and aimed more at permitting givers a sense of participation.

The Ministerial League met that night at about 7:00 at St. Mark Methodist Church.

> Our church is the basic meeting place for the Ministerial League. Other meetings are always special. This is at the call of the group in order that we might have this feeling of location, headquarters . . . they kind of like to have. . . . We had, I would say, something like twenty pastors. The original meeting that was held was simply to ask the pastors to come because there is a disaster. Do we have a responsibility was the question that I asked. The answer was certainly that we have a responsibility. We did establish four or five committees. The need of one committee was the Red Cross liaison. This committee was connected to the Red Cross to see exactly what is available. This is because it has already been said that the Red Cross would put people in a house. We need to know what did they really mean by this. An Air Force liaison committee was established because this $1,000 business and then another committee was established, the Legal Aid Committee. What is a person really to do in a situation like this nature and . . . . The particular responsibility of the ministers on the committees was to either work with the person who had information or they were to get information themselves. But they would only get the information if they thought they were qualified. Now, put this this way, to define our Legal Aid committee. We do not attempt to give anyone any legal advice. We do try to tell the people that you need legal advice. We then try to contact some

attorneys and say, "Will you be available to give advice to these people?" and letting them know the areas concerned about.

The establishing of these committees was an effort that these people who are affected by the disaster might have an opportunity to get some information. There are four committees; the last committee—let's see; Red Cross, Air Force, Legal Aid, and location. Now location was if there were persons coming out of the disaster might want to relocate elsewhere, could we be any help as a minister's group. The group had a good bit of activity. They went out and began gathering information; the Air Force was very cooperative, very cooperative indeed. The Red Cross was very cooperative. When at one time the air was most polluted with misinformation and the Air Force and Red Cross were asked to meet with the Ministerial League, they did so very kindly. This was probably three, four, maybe five days after the disaster itself. They met with the group. We had probably again twenty-odd pastors present. We met with Colonel Trask, Captain Morton of the Air Force, and the disaster chairman of Red Cross. We met, we went over as a ministerial group with these persons, the things that were our concerns. For example, in terms of following forms, a person comes in and files a form. Does this person know that the Air Force is going to do all that they can to protect the Air Force and this is probably proper and right. The question is, as they would attempt to do this, are they in any way interfering with the life of this individual who may feel they have a just claim. This is something that we as pastors couldn't answer at all. This is where our legal aid department comes in. If this person has a question, don't ask your pastor; he's not an attorney, he doesn't know. But your pastor would want you to see an attorney.

A number of people found it natural to go to their ministers to seek material aid. Some persons found it natural to give to ministers of their acquaintance, rather than through normal institutional channels. The result was that the Ministerial League found itself in the money-collecting and dispensing business.

> Some families don't know anything about the Red Cross at all; all they had was hearsay. And someone says the Red Cross won't treat you right. I'm not going to pay the Red Cross; they don't give you anything anyway. We tried to tell them to go to the ministerial. So if this person really had a need, we felt that this is where we might be of service. This family who wants to contribute, but their whole basic nature does not let them support a community organization. And a family needs help but their basic nature will not allow them to go to a community agency, but they will come to their pastor. They will come to the Ministerial League. So that's what we did, we did acquire approximately three hundred dollars. The three hundred dollars acquired was distributed to families. On a Sunday afternoon, I cannot recall the exact Sunday, either the second or third Sunday of February, this happened the sixteenth of January? I believe it was the first Sunday in February, I believe it was, we sent out a letter to as many of the people as we had the names that were in the disaster itself. We invited them to Tabernacle Church where we wanted to make a community report on the activities of the Ministerial League. There was a one hundred dollar balance at the time of the meeting and as president, I said "I do not want to leave this meeting with a dime of the disaster money. I must close out right now." Now this group I asked, "Are there any families you know that need help, that have not been able to have this need met through the Red Cross or Air Force in a monetary way?" There were two families brought to our attention that time. I don't recall their names exactly, but my records will show this. And the money was then officially voted out and the account was closed.

The crash seemed to have a significant impact upon church attendance the following morning.

> Well, it's true that the services were really crowded. They felt that many of the questions were, "Why did God have this happen?" Did I think that this was really an act of God?—this kind of thing. Many people are prone to whenever a disaster occurs, that this is the work of the Lord. And of course my very frequent answer was that no, this was the work of men. The errors of men will cause much disaster and how we can relate this to God is something beyond me. I think there are many passages of Scripture that you could use to do almost anything that you really wanted to prove, but I simply laid this on the errors of men that they made a mistake somewhere along the line in the aircraft and it's being checked out. And then I know that they have quite a magnitude to check out but at the best times, men have gone astray. It was a full house that Sunday.

Again and again such conversations return to the point of communication, and to the fact that "we cannot overlook the fact that this is a Negro community. The Air Force is white. The Red Cross is white."

> Imagine the position of the common layman going in and being talked to in such a way in compiling these reports that he gets all confused. You want me to sign something and I don't want to sign it. Now on the outside the people are saying, "I hope that they're different from other white men." I have heard or read that I might get $1,000 but I don't believe it. I know I can't get it. So I am supposed to trust this man who says I might get $1,000 on the radio and when I go to him he tells me no. They tell me this, of all things: "We cannot give you any money. Go to the Red Cross." Now, to me, as a Negro, who doesn't have much confidence in the white man—I have come in because my house has been damaged and I need help and they are going to give me a third degree about getting what appears due me. There is the feeling that you wouldn't do this if it were out on another [i.e., white] street. What kind of treatment would they have given it if it would have been in another area?

There were rumors and questions in the Negro community. Had the pilot tried to nose the plane into the empty lot near which he crashed? Why was the plane flying over that area of town? Could the pilot and/or crew have preferred that area for crash purposes rather than another? Had they any choice? These need not be rhetorical questions. The Air Force seems to suggest that there was no element of pilot choice in the place or moment of impact. Many in the Negro community give equivocal answers to these questions. "One of the Air Force persons said to me, 'Why, you don't think that plane really meant to do this, do you?' It was a guilt thing that someone had mentioned. It bothered him enough that he came and asked me. I said to him that I hope—certainly hope—that we have no nuts flying for us. This is my answer because I hope nobody is going to deliberately . . . turn a plane to the ground to get themself a few people."

The absence of houses on both sides of North Piatt is no longer so oppressive. The sites have been leveled, and the grass has grown back. Those who have stayed live the same kinds of life, work at the same kinds of occupation, trade in the same kind of business community. Their children attend and drop out of the same schools. The moderate-militant leadership dichotomy which the *Beacon* found to exist probably is as valid an identification of community leadership as any in Newark, Detroit, Milwaukee, and other cities where rioting has occurred.

There was talk of the city acquiring the sites of the destroyed homes, and constructing park facilities with some kind of memorial to the victims. This has passed, and the grassy lots at present promise to be a memorial to the crash for the indefinite future. New construction is not in prospect.

The KC-135's and B-52's still arch westward on take-off from McConnell, but this is no more threat to the people of the ghetto than to residents of other neighborhoods in Wichita which fall within the flight patterns for landing or take-off. It is reasonable to expect that another military plane will come down some day. This, like holiday weekend traffic tolls, passenger plane crashes, and the casualty lists from South Vietnam, is a "normal" consequence of the civilization we have built and of the times in which we live. It is one of the risks of living.

VIII

The Aftermath

> "Of course, there is no way to compensate or repay the families who have suffered these tragic losses. However, the least we can do is settle the claims as fairly and as quickly as possible."[1]

Until 1946, one of the more significant anomalies in our system of responsible government was the persistence of the rule, derivative from the era of monarchical absolutism in England, that the subject may not sue the sovereign—that is, without the permission of the sovereign. Analogizing from the relationship between the sixteenth- and seveteenth-century English subject and his king, to that between the twentieth-century American citizen and the federal government, the United States applied this rule until the passage of the Federal Tort Claims Act of 1946.[2] The standard and cumbersome way around the rule was to persuade a member of Congress to introduce private legislation, either granting redress for alleged harm worked upon a citizen by an agent of the government or granting permission to sue in the federal courts.

In addition to the Federal Tort Claims Act, the Military Claims Act of 1943 permits the military to settle administratively and pay certain claims for damage to or loss of property and for personal injury or death. As restated in the U.S. Code, a continuously updated compendium of congressional enactments, the Judge Advocate General of each service is permitted, under regulations established by the secretary of his service department, to "settle and pay in an amount not more than $5,000 a claim against the United States for—(1) damage to, or loss of, real property . . . ; (2) damage to, or loss of, personal property . . . ; or (3) personal injury or death; either caused by a civilian officer or employee of that department, or a member of the Army, Navy, Air Force, or Marine Corps, as the case may be, acting within the scope of his employment, or otherwise incident to noncombat activities of that department."[3] A claim must be presented in writing within two years. The secretary of a military department may approve a claim in excess of $5,000 if he finds it meritorious, but may pay only $5,000 of it, reporting "the excess to Congress for its consideration. In any case where the amount to be paid is not more than $1,000, . . . any officer of an armed force under the jurisdiction of the department concerned" may be delegated authority to settle it. All claims prosecuted and paid through this administrative procedure are to be considered finally settled; no further legal recourse against the government is available.[4] In July and August, 1961, immediately preceding the fatal Air Force crash of August 25 in Midwest City, Oklahoma, the two Houses of Congress considered legislation which became law on September 8, permitting the military for the first time to advance emergency funds up to $1,000 to persons injured or suffering property loss or damage, or the death of relatives resulting from military aircraft or missile crashes.[5]

Shortly after the crash in Wichita, Representative Garner E. Shriver of the Fourth District, Kansas, within which McConnell Air Force Base and Wichita are located, introduced legislation to lift the $5,000 limit on administrative settlement of claims arising from the January 16 crash. The House Judiciary Committee Report, which accompanied and recommended passage of Shriver's bill, pointed out that such legislation would be consonant with previous enactments of the Eighty-seventh Congress covering the Midwest City crash and of the Eighty-sixth Congress covering a crash at Little Rock, Arkansas, in early 1960. Secretary of the Air Force Eugene M. Zuckert supported the bill, which was adopted by Congress and became law when approved by the President July 7.[6]

Public Law 89-65 lifts the $5,000 limit for administrative settlement of claims for the January 16, 1965, Wichita crash, requires that the Secretary of the Air Force "within thirty months after the enactment of this Act, report to Congress" on all claims settled and all claims filed but remaining unsettled under the Act, and restricts attorney's fees to a maximum of 10 per cent of any recovery under the Act. It also provides that payments "shall not be subject to insurance subrogation claims in any respect." In simple language, claimants were to receive all proceeds, less attorney fees not to exceed 10 per cent of the settlement amount, while insurance companies which had already made payment on policies could not recover from the settlement proceeds. Violation of the 10 per cent limitation on attorney fees is declared a misdemeanor subject to a fine "not exceeding $1,000."

The individual states tend to place a statutory ceiling upon the valuation of human life, preventing recovery of more than a specified amount for wrongful death. Federal authorities observe the limits thus set. In 1965, the Kansas wrongful death statute limited recovery to $25,000 plus "reasonable funeral expenses," and "expenses for the care of the deceased."[7] With this in mind, and estimating twenty-two civilian deaths, seventeen injuries including four hospitalizations, plus destruction of twelve private homes and damage to seventy-five others, the Air Force anticipated "a total of 125 claims resulting from the crash, and there is a possibility of an additional 60 more being filed." Total settlements, it said, might run to $300,000, under the Act.[8] This estimate must have been thrown together somewhat casually. Even conceding that state court judgments in wrongful death cases vary according to age, health, and wage-earner status of the deceased, if one halved the $550,000 maximum recovery for twenty-two wrongful deaths under Kansas law and proceeded to build, on that figure, estimates for personal injury and property loss, the result would vastly exceed $300,000. Indeed, subsequent suits, administrative settlements, and settlements out of court cause the Air Force estimate to appear totally inadequate.

Immediately following the crash,

> A permanent command post was established in an abandoned grocery store [in a shopping complex between Minneapolis and Minnesota on the South side of 21st Street]. The store's plate glass window, removed for

> storage, was quickly replaced by glaziers who had been working on another building across the street. Lumber for partitions was rushed from McConnell.
>
> Colonel James E. Trask, McConnell Air Force Base Commander, was relieved of his air base duties to take charge of the command post and await the arrival of Gen. David Wade, Second Air Force Commander. . . .
>
> Telephone and electric company repairmen were among the first to reach the crash area. While streets were still filled with the burning fuel, emergency lines were strung to the temporary command post. . . . Five days after the tragic event, the lights still burned late into the night at the command post at 21st and Piatt.
>
> Air Force representatives, assisted by the Red Cross, are busily providing emergency assistance and processing claims. Typewriters pound into the night telling the story of people rebuilding their lives.
>
> It's a story of cooperative effort, of military men and civilians bound closer together by the ties of tragedy.[9]

The Air Force Judge Advocate General (JAG) immediately authorized the staff judge advocate at McConnell to make emergency payments up to $1,000 each "to alleviate hardship of the injured and homeless." He was also authorized to make final settlement in the field for all claims presented for $1,000 or less. In the February 24, 1965, House Report on the Shriver Bill, the Air Force reported that "a total of $8,990.59 in emergency payments has been made. Five small claims in a total amount of approximately $200 have been settled and paid. The total of all claims or requests for emergency payments which have been received is 56." Five special Air Force investigative teams were organized to expedite settlement of claims. An "experienced private civilian appraiser" was employed "for the purpose of appraising damage to the destroyed realty," and the Corps of Engineers estimated repair costs for houses not completely destroyed.

In a report submitted to Representative Garner E. Shriver, April 20, 1967, the Air Force indicated that of 232 claims filed for administrative settlement, 172 were paid; $640,072.59 in claims were settled for $104,765.97, and an additional $8,990.59

was expended in the form of twenty-two emergency payments. Forty-six claims were disapproved and fifteen withdrawn. Of all these claims, only one individual hurt by the crash—Harvey Dale, who lost his forty-seven-year-old wife and two-year-old daughter and whose home and contents were destroyed—received a settlement in excess of the $5,000 limitation of the Military Claims Act. This was for $36,840.38, and made on December 22, 1965. Six other settlements in excess of $5,000 were made, one to the Gas Service Company for damage to its distribution system, one to the city of Wichita for damage to property, and four to insurance companies.[10]

The McConnell Air Force Base JAG office investigates and processes claims in excess of $1,000, forwarding the claim and recommendations to Oklahoma Air Material Area (OCAMA) at Tinker Air Force Base, Oklahoma. OCAMA must in turn forward claims in excess of $2,500 to Air Force Logistics Command, Wright-Patterson Air Force Base, Dayton, Ohio; and those in excess of $5,000 must go to the Air Force JAG in Washington. This review process resulted in a substantial reduction in the settlement with Harvey Dale, as proposed by the McConnell JAG office. It resulted, also, in a very unhappy claimant.

The observer of these activities is left with an impression of well-intentioned, gargantuan efforts by the Air Force, which afforded such slight relief compared to the magnitude of the harm committed and the need existing that the enterprise was cloaked in an aura of beneficent bureaucratic busywork. In any event, though the extent of the Air Force's efforts seemed adequate to its responsible personnel, those efforts were misunderstood and somewhat unappreciated by those to whom they were directed.

The gap between Air Force effort and community perception of results is evidenced by an August 5, 1965, *Wichita Eagle* story captioned "KC-135 Crash Hardships Linger." The tone of the story is established in the first sentence: "Money is not a sure cure for heartaches, but many of the surviving victims of a KC-135 crash in northeast Wichita have had to go without funds while patching up their wounded bodies and homes." It then narrates several instances of alleged procrastination or dilatoriness on the part of the Air Force in affording relief to claimants. From the

Air Force point of view, claims settlement stemming from the disaster, although taking precedence over all other claims, was nonetheless, "a painstaking, time-consuming task and the staff is handling it with as much speed as possible."[11]

Disaster victims were told by several sources to seek advice from an attorney prior to signing a final settlement. Indeed, the reluctance of many victims to sign any document for fear of surrendering rights posed difficulties for JAG officers who in the first days following the crash probably had a positive incentive to pay out money, if only they could find victims and persuade them to provide documentation and execute forms. The author has corroboration of one instance in which an Air Force JAG officer literally carried a $1,000 check to a hospital and pressed it upon a reluctant but needy recipient who feared its acceptance would jeopardize his claim. Attorneys in some cases advised their clients to litigate rather than to pursue administrative settlement procedures. Other claimants converted their claims to suits after becoming dissatisfied with Air Force processing. Major Cordingly, quoted above, reported sixteen such instances as of the end on September, 1965. There is in Air Force JAG circles a prevalent and plausible belief that attorneys advised litigation in lieu of administrative settlement because of the vast difference between the 20 per cent fee permitted under the Federal Tort Claims Act and the 10 per cent allowed under P.L. 89-65. The Air Force was reportedly set to work processing other claims which were filed only to permit their dramatic withdrawal with attendant publicity.

This Air Force JAG attitude is shared by the assistant U.S. attorney representing the government in the Federal Tort Claims actions. He sees significance in the sequence of events leading to litigation.

> The chronology of these events may be illuminating. The special litigation [sic] of Rep. Shriver became law in early July 1965. Mr. Lewis [Chester I. Lewis, who represented many of the claimants] dismissed his claims in late July and filed his lawsuits in early August. Most of the lawsuits now on file were filed after the passage of the legislation. It is, I suppose, a fit subject for specula-

> tion that the decision on the part of these attorneys to proceed by lawsuit, rather than administrative claim, may have been influenced by the fact that Congress inserted in the special legislation a limitation on attorneys' fees to ten percent of the recovered amount, whereas the allowable attorney's fee under Federal Tort claims litigation is twenty-five percent [it was actually 20 per cent in 1965, going up to 25 per cent in January, 1967].[12]

Assistant U.S. Attorney Guy L. Goodwin takes the position that "a very simple administrative claim procedure existed for quick relief of these claimants.... It is difficult to understand why all claimants with bona fide claims did not avail themselves of this procedure. It is even more difficult to understand why attorneys would advise their clients to pursue the route of adversary litigation, which they knew would be lengthy by its very nature, when this short and speedy route was available. It is even more unusual that Mr. Lewis . . . would abandon administrative claims on behalf of his clients *before they had been acted upon,* in favor of lengthy litigation."[13]

Not even the Air Force pretends that its claims procedure is "simple," "short and speedy," although experience certainly confirms that it is more expeditious than litigation. This author, however, is not competent to assess the propriety of an attorney's recommending litigation rather than administrative proceedings where the government has made the option available.

Undoubtedly there was some basis for attorneys attributing to the Air Force the necessity for litigation. The *Wichita Eagle* reported on August 14, 1965, that attorney Chester I. Lewis had that week filed eight separate suits in the U.S. District Court for recovery of injuries and damages to survivors or relatives of survivors of the January crash.

> Lewis said he originally sought recovery through claims submitted to the claims office at McConnell Air Force Base here. Most of the claims were submitted in May and June. The Air Force never acknowledged receipt of the claims, he said.
>
> Because of the lack of response on the claims, he decided to withdraw them and file suits in court for re-

covery. Lewis said he hopes to get more action and quicker settlements through the court.

The suits contend the Air Force was negligent and therefore liable for injuries and damages in the crash. . . .

Lewis said that by suing for recovery he hopes to gain access to the accident report to determine causes of the crash.

"I think public policy would dictate that they (the Air Force) disclose what the cause was," he said. "This has nothing to do with military security or national defense."[14]

Lewis, who ultimately was to handle ten, or one-third of the thirty cases filed, is a Negro, President of the Wichita NAACP, and active in race relations movements. G. Edmond Hayes, another Wichita attorney and a Negro, had earlier filed suit on behalf of Mr. and Mrs. George Meyers for $132,000. "The Meyers escaped their burning home at 2027 N. Piatt with their young daughters, severely burning their feet as they raced through the flames."[15] By February, 1966, twenty-one suits had been filed in U.S. District Court involving claims aggragating in excess of 1 million dollars.[16] More would come. A list of plaintiffs and claims procured from District Court in March, 1967, showed thirty suits involving claims totalling $1,068,761.36.

The Boeing Company was named co-defendant in six of the suits in a motion filed by Chester I. Lewis in October, 1965. Upon a reading of the Air Force investigation report, to which he had been granted access, Lewis, according to the *Wichita Beacon,* had concluded:

That the tanker "was of dangerous and defective design. Evidence clearly shows that the crash of said tanker was due to violent severe power rudder 'deflection.' "

That Boeing "neither in its flight handbook nor otherwise informed the defendant (the Air Force) . . . of the flight characteristics or procedures to be followed in actual flight if a power rudder has a severe deflection as it did in the case herein."

That Boeing failed "to test and determine compatibility of component parts of the airplane."[17]

It would appear that the Air Force investigation report, copies of which were made available to plaintiffs' attorneys, does not draw conclusions concerning the cause of the crash. Wichitans were informed in February, 1967, that these conclusions were to be found in a "secret" Air Force investigative report. Attorney Terry O'Keefe, co-counsel for all of the plaintiffs, argued in pretrial conference and before the District Court that this report was "the crux of the case."

"U.S. Assistant District Attorney Guy L. Goodwin, representing the government, said the government does not 'concede such a report does exist. I have no knowledge that it does exist . . . therefore I must deny it.' "[18] On Monday, March 27, 1967, Judge Wesley E. Brown of the U.S. District Court ordered the government and the Boeing Company to make available to the plaintiffs the findings of the "secret" report, existence of which had been denied on behalf of the government a month earlier.[19] The morning *Eagle* commented on Judge Brown's ruling: "In a ruling Monday, Judge Brown ordered the U.S. government and codefendant, The Boeing Co., to make available to plaintiffs all factual findings regarding the crash, including the major portion of the official Air Force accident investigation report.

"Not included in the order were conclusions drawn by the official board as to the probable cause of the crash and recommendations for correcting the cause."

The U.S. district judge did, however, keep open the possibility of making these conclusions available to plaintiffs if the factual findings in the report were not sufficiently informative.[20]

Guy L. Goodwin points out that the government "at the outset made available for inspection and copying all factual portions of the voluminous report of the [Air Force] Collateral Board which investigated this accident." In his opinion, while the remarks attributed to him above "were true" they were made "in connection with a request of a thirty-day continuance until the proper attorney for the Department of Justice in Washington, D.C., who would know of the existence of any such report, would be present." Perhaps, as Mr. Goodwin suggests, "the inaccurate reporting of the local newspapers" is responsible for impressions that the government was being devious, if not deceitful, in its representations concerning the "secret" report. In any event, when "it was learned that the report referred to as the 'secret' report was the Accident/Incident Investigation Report, . . . pertinent portions of this report were *voluntarily given* to all counsel for the plaintiffs." Thus, according to this source, the report was provided to counsel prior to Judge Brown's order of March 27, 1967, formalizing their entitlement to it.[21]

Two months after these events, Wichitans learned that eight of the thirty suits had been settled out of court. These were among the ten suits filed by Lewis, who "indicated he would take no further action against The Boeing Co., which was named as codefendant in the cases. 'My clients and I are pleased. I hope the government is also,' Lewis said."[22] These suits included that of Alvin T. Allen, who had sued for $22,049.15 and settled for $8,000; Mr. and Mrs. Clarence Walker, who sought $39,409.95 and, to their disgruntlement, received $37,000 for personal injury and property damage; Marguerite and Talmadge Shaw, who received $28,059 of $49,959.73 sought for the estate of Mr. and Mrs. Albert L. Bolden and child who died at 2053 N. Piatt; Laura Lee Randolph, who received $18,175 of $39,737.56 claimed as a result of the disaster which took five lives, including that of her daughter Tracy, at 2037 N. Piatt; Henderson Kye, who received $2,500 of $25,215.40 sought for the death of his wife, a victim of a stroke resulting from the crash; the Reverend U. W. Barron, who received $9,000 of $13,482.63 claimed for injuries and property damage at 2054 N. Piatt; and two cases in which administrators for the estates of six persons who died at 2041 N. Piatt settled for a total of $56,569 of $97,321.05 sought. Attorney's fees as reported in the press amounted to about 20 per cent of the settlements.

These settlements represented a total compromise from $287,175.47 claimed to $159,303 received—approximately 59 per cent of the amount for which the individuals sued. Admittedly these are not typical Federal Tort Claims Act cases. Indeed, in the year ending June 30, 1965, the Department of Justice settled 731 tort cases after suit had been instituted, in which the claims totaled 24 million dollars but were settled for a total of 6 million dollars. This is a settlement record of 25¢ on the dollar for the government, as contrasted to 59¢ on the dollar in the Wichita cases. In that same year, the 169 judgments under the Federal Tort Claims Act totaled approximately 4 million dollars against 24 million dollars claimed, or about 17¢ on the dollar.[23] We have only one Wichita Air Force administrative settlement of an individual's claim in excess of $5,000 against which to make comparison, and there, the amount originally *claimed* is not available—we only know that the settlement permitted after review was substantially below that *recommended* by the lowest echelon Air Force JAG involved. That settlement was paid in December, 1965, and thus the claimant benefited in terms of expedition, if not finance, by processing his claim administratively. Five claims on which the Air Force made settlement as a result of the Midwest City, Oklahoma crash were paid at the rate of 59¢ per dollar claimed.[24] Twelve claims filed under P.L. 86-476, covering the Little Rock crash, were settled administratively at the rate of 37¢ on the dollar claimed. In addition to these, 526 of 560 claims presented under the Military Claims Act (administrative settlement of claims up to $5,000) were approved for settlement in full or in part, at the settlement rate of 80¢ per dollar claimed.[25] Even this information is fragmentary in relation to the total claims settlement activity, and we do not have additional collected data to provide an adequate basis for comparison of the results of judicial and administrative claims procedures.[26] It is interesting, whether or not significant, that these administrative settlements averaged the same as the out-of-court settlements in Wichita.

We have come to a point at which evaluation of purpose, procedure, and performance is required.

Lt. Colonel J. W. Scanlan of the Office of Deputy Chief of Staff, Personnel, Department of the Air Force, testified before the Senate Committee on Armed Services in support of the 1961 legislation permitting the military to advance money (up to $1,000) to persons harmed by the crash of a plane or missile.

> The operation of aircraft or missiles of the military departments occasionally results in accidents which cause damage to private property and injury or death to civilians.

When such accidents occur, there is almost always an urgent need by the damaged party for funds for certain expenses. In cases where homes are destroyed, there exists the problem of buying new clothes, obtaining meals at restaurants, and arranging for shelter at hotels. Emergency repairs are usually required to make damaged buildings habitable or at least to protect them from further deterioration from exposure to the elements.

> At present there is no authority which the military services can use to provide immediate financial assistance when required. The victims of the accidents are advised of their right to file claims. This is ordinarily a lengthy process. In some cases, the damaged parties have been forced to rely upon public charities or the charity of friends and neighbors. The usually spectacular nature of these disasters focuses public attention and magnifies the problem. The lack of authority for the services to satisfy immediately the obligations arising from aircraft accidents invites widespread adverse publicity with accompanying loss of public confidence. It is felt that favorable consideration of this proposal is justified for human reasons as well as to fulfill moral obligations.[27]

The House Committee on Armed Services, in favorably reporting the proposed legislation, referred to the relative inability of the military to provide immediate relief after the 1960 explosion of an Air Force jet bomber over Little Rock, Arkansas. "A principal part of the airplane fell in three sections of the city with flaming debris being scattered over a wide area. In this case, six homes were totally destroyed. There were 24 homes with major structural damage and over 100 additional homes with minor damage. There were two civilian deaths and several cases of minor injuries. As soon as notification was received, the Air Force opened a claims office in the city hall to answer questions, to help in presentation of claims, and to do everything possible to alleviate distress. There was, however, no authority to provide immediate financial assistance which certainly would have been appropriate to those persons rendered homeless in this accident."[28] In the case of the Midwest City crash, which followed this committee report by a month, the Air Force, lacking authority to offer financial aid to the two injured civilians, took the initiative of evacuating them to the Lackland Air Force Base Hospital, San Antonio, Texas, for specialized treatment for their burns.[29]

We begin, then, with the assumption—charitable, some will say—that the overriding concern of the military and the Congress in domestic, noncombat military disasters, is to alleviate the distress of those affected and to provide such material restitution as is physically possible, promptly, fairly, charitably, and without captious bureaucratic quibbling. Certainly it is a bizarre contradiction of this purpose and of the reasoning behind the 1961 legislation for the Air Force to refer those persons it has dislocated to the Red Cross or other agencies where they must demonstrate their need and then accept such relief as that agency regards suitable, when it has authority to advance funds to enable individuals to determine and fill their own recuperative needs.

It was a travesty of the whole intent, attributed, perhaps wrongly, to Congress, for such crash victims to be so treated by the military that they sought redress instead under the Federal Tort Claims Act. Accurate as Colonel Scanlan's reference to the "lengthy process" associated with Air Force claims may be, the judicial route to recovery can be longer yet. G. Edmond Hayes, Wichita attorney for at least one of the plaintiffs in the KC-135 suit, reported to the *Wichita Eagle* on page one of the August 5, 1965 issue:

> I have just received a rather curious letter from Guy Goodwin, the U.S. district attorney here, which makes me wonder what is up. . . .
>
> The letter reads in part:
>
> "In formal conversations with the court it has been indicated that all of the lawsuits arising out of this aircraft crash might be consolidated for the purposes of trial on the question of liability, with a subsequent hearing on the matter of damages.

"This would mean, of course, that the court would wait until the expiration of the two-year statute of limitations before consolidating the cases and setting them for trial. Obviously considerable time would elapse after that before they reach a final disposition."

The *Eagle* story concluded, "Hayes says all he can assume from the communication is that he is being pressured to make a much lower settlement out of court."[30] Hayes' interpretation of the purpose behind the government attorney's letter may be correct. The implication of a two-year delay in litigation which Goodwin finds in Judge Wesley E. Brown's alleged intention to consolidate the cases, however, does not necessarily bear up under scrutiny. There was no reason why one case could not become the vehicle for determining liability, so that the resultant decision would set a precedent for succeeding cases filed before the two-year statute of limitations, which would require only a determination of appropriate damages in their proceedings. Presumably, there was no reason why attorneys for plaintiffs could not so argue before the judge, in an effort to expedite placing the cases on a trial docket. In fact, counsel for the government and for the plaintiffs, and indeed the Court, appeared to have no interest in expediting trial. While the *Wichita Eagle* in February, 1966, reported that Boeing was ready for trial, it simultaneously reported that "counsel for the government and for the plaintiffs said they were not." The Court did not anticipate early trial: " 'These cases are not old,' Judge Brown said. 'They are among the newest on our docket.

" 'Naturally the claimants are anxious and they have a right to a hearing. We will take these cases in their proper order and dispose of them as soon as all parties are ready.' "[31]

In late July, 1967, the author was informed by the clerk of the U.S. District Court that "all of these cases are still pending and as yet no trial date has been set."[32]

It is not the author's purpose to suggest that any person or group of persons has been dilatory in handling these cases, but rather to make the point that litigation is not an expeditious route to affording relief to those damaged under the circumstances involved in these cases. The assistant U.S. attorney, who is quoted earlier on the inevitability of protracted proceedings in court, quite properly points out that, as is indicated above on the basis of newspaper reports, all of the attorneys involved in the cases asked for or agreed to the stay of proceedings until expiration of the two-year statute of limitations.

> Recognizing the possible delay inherent in the litigation approach, and the consolidation procedure adopted by the Court, it is difficult to understand how the government or the undersigned could be held responsible for any delay in processing of valid claims arising out of this disaster. Responsibility for a great portion of the delay after the commencement of this litigation was due, in fact, to the actions of attorneys for all of the plaintiffs. It was on the written motion of *all counsel for the plaintiffs,* requesting that all proceedings in the cases be stayed until after the statute of limitations had run (two years) that the Court ordered a stay of proceedings. . . . [Furthermore,] all of the attorneys involved knew that civil litigation in the U.S. District Court at Wichita, Kansas, is hampered by a crowded docket and delay is inevitable. It was that condition which prompted the recent appointment of a new Judge for this District."[33]

Disregarding inevitable delay in the judicial process and the question of whether or not it is reasonable for the trial court to wait until all the suits are filed before proceeding to establish liability, there remains the vital issue of whether Congress wishes to put the unwitting and unwilling victims of our defense effort in a position in which, to recoup such losses as can be translated into monetary terms, they must enter into gladiatorial combat with their government.[34] How else is one to describe a contest characterized by such episodes as secret reports whose existence is denied by the attorney for the government, but which the government subsequently is ordered to make available to plaintiffs?

Public Law 89-65 should be ample evidence to its author and to Congress of the inadequacy of this approach to affording relief to the victims of noncombat military disasters. Little of practical value to the human beings directly touched by the disaster was accomplished by eliminating the $5,000 ceiling for administrative settlement of claims. At this juncture it is relevant to note that Wichitans who had observed the tedious process of administrative or judicial restitution to victims of the January, 1965 crash were dismayed at the seeming alacrity and liberality characterizing settlements with victims of such crashes abroad.[35] A reading of Title 10 U.S. Code Sec. 2734 should relieve the Air Force of criticism for this disparity in paying claims for damage or loss of property, personal injury, or death. The Code opens with the words, "To promote and maintain friendly relations through the prompt settlement of meritorious claims, the Secretary concerned or any officer designated by him may . . . appoint one or more claims commissions, each composed of one or more commissioned officers of the armed forces under his jurisdiction, to settle and pay any claim for not more than $15,000."

The purpose of Section 2734 is clear and unimpeachable. Foreign nations have leverage which must be recognized. If liberality ($15,000 rather than $5,000 maximum for administrative settlement) and expedition (perhaps effected by the "claims commissions") in settling claims resulting from a crash such as that which occurred in Wichita, help to maintain good relations with other countries, these are commendable congressional policies.

At the same time, it is not being parochial or xenophobic to suggest that steps should be taken to secure the same liberal treatment for Americans. The Air Force, which had the humaneness to petition Congress in 1961 for permission to advance monetary help to crash victims, is singularly lacking in this quality, or in making it felt, when it comes to dealing with victims following a crash. Perhaps it feels the breath of the Comptroller General on its neck. Perhaps it feels that parsimonious settlement of such claims, with such petty and seemingly petulant regard for documentation that administrative settlement becomes an adversary process, will find favor with Congress. Perhaps it feels it is better to provide incentive for opting judicial settlement. These attitudes may filter down to the officer on the paying line, whose concern for approbation of his performance leads him to emulate the institutional qualities described above.

On July 18, 1966, an amendment to the Federal Tort Claims Act was signed into law, to take effect January 18, 1967.[36] It promises to radically alter the method of handling claims against the government from that which prevailed at the time of the crash and has been characterized in this chapter. The new Act requires that claimants attempt settlement with the responsible agency of the government prior to instituting suit. Expeditious administrative settlement is encouraged by a provision of the statute freeing claimants to take their cases to court if the agency fails to settle within six months of the filing of the claim.

Agency heads may settle claims for amounts up to $25,000, and may make higher settlements "with the prior written approval of the Attorney General or his designee" for each such case. Attorney fees are adjusted enough to virtually eliminate the possibility of an attorney holding out for litigation over administrative settlement because of higher fees. Attorney fees may be as high as 20 per cent of the administrative settlement, or, if the case goes to court, 25 per cent of the recovery. Since the attorney has no option but to go through the procedure of administrative effort to settle a claim, he would be foolish to take on the additional burden of litigation for the trivial incentive of an extra five per cent. Were the prospects for a significantly greater settlement bright, it might be in the claimant's interest to litigate. We have already seen, however, that Federal Tort Claims settlements are not great in relation to the amounts sought. The new procedure also eliminates the need for referring claims settlements to Congress for supplemental appropriations action.

The two principal provisions of the new law are:

> The head of each Federal agency or his designee, in accordance with regulations prescribed by the Attorney General, may consider, ascertain, adjust, determine, compromise, and settle any claim for money damages against the United States for injury or loss of property or personal injury or death caused by the negligent or wrongful act or omission of any employee of the agency while acting within the scope of his office or employment, under circumstances where the United States, if a private person, would be liable to the claimant in ac-

cordance with the law of the place where the act or omission occurred: *Provided,* That any award, compromise, or settlement in excess of $25,000 shall be effected only with the prior written approval of the Attorney General or his designee.

An action shall not be instituted upon a claim against the United States for money damages for injury or loss of property or personal injury or death caused by the negligent or wrongful act or omission of any employee of the Government while acting within the scope of his office or employment, unless the claimant shall have first presented the claim to the appropriate Federal agency and his claim shall have been finally denied by the agency in writing and sent by certified or registered mail. The failure of an agency to make final disposition of a claim within six months after it is filed shall, at the option of the claimant any time thereafter, be deemed a final denial of the claim for purposes of this section. The provisions of this subsection shall not apply to such claims as may be asserted under the Federal Rules of Civil Procedure by third party complaint, cross-claim, or counterclaim.

Before rejoicing at the enactment of the new law, however, let us first review the consideration of it in Senate and House committees. The Senate Judiciary Committee either held no hearing or printed none. Subcommittee No. 2 of the House Judiciary Committee heard testimony on four related proposals for amendment to the Federal Tort Claims Act, presented by the Justice Department. The thirty-five pages of "hearing" consist of the texts of the four bills, a formal communication to the Speaker of the House from Attorney General Nicholas Katzenbach, and testimony and a statement by Assistant Attorney General John W. Douglas.[37] One principal concern of Mr. Douglas was to express the Justice Department's willingness to go along with the preference of Senator Sam J. Ervin, Jr. (N.C.), who introduced the bills in the Senate, for reducing the ceiling for administrative settlement from the $50,000 originally proposed by Justice to the $25,000 stipulated in the Act. "The $25,000 figure would permit agency authority to settle cases by itself in 90 per cent of the cases which are now settled by the Justice Department after suit. In addition, $25,000 embraces 75 per cent of the judgments which are eventually rendered if settlement is out of the question in court suits."[38] A second concern was to persuade the committee members that administrative settlement of claims would lower costs for processing claims and yield lower awards. "Of the 731 settlements entered into by the Department in Fiscal 1965, the average settlement was just under 7% of the claim. On the other hand, in the 169 judgments against the Government, the average reward was slightly more than 17% of the claim."[39] These arguments concerning lower settlements to claimants and consequent savings to the government are flanked, in Mr. Douglas' presentation, by arguments stressing the need for reducing court congestion and the satisfactions for both claimants and government in early disposition of claims.

It is fair to assume that the bulk of tort claims against the military, resulting from noncombat domestic accidents, will in the future be settled according to the procedures outlined above. This is a substantial achievement. It removes the citizen claimant from a situation in which he must enter into an arena of combat where he is pitted against a skilled U.S. attorney, who performs an extremely important and worthy function prosecuting alleged criminals and representing the government in civil cases—an adversary whose professional qualifications are likely to be judged by his score of "wins." In a Federal Tort Claim Act case, a win for the government is either a judgment against a claimant or the smallest possible judgment. This is a process for accomplishing a purpose quite divergent from that stressed by Senator Monroney in the headnote to this chapter.

But this is not enough. With particular reference to the Air Force JAG, the Pentagon should include a flying squad of three to five attorneys, headed by a person of at least the rank of colonel. In the event of an accident involving property damage, personal injury, or death to civilians, one or more of these officers should be dispatched to the scene. There, enlisting as necessary the aid of JAG officers from the nearest Air Force facility, the Washington officers should conduct on-the-spot visual review of the damage, take testimony on the nature and extent of the damage, and attempt to negotiate final settlements with injured parties and their attorneys. A case involving damage worked by military aircraft should be settled within a matter of days or weeks, rather than months or years, and with a minimum of review by officials remote from the accident. In order to accomplish this in consistency with present law, it might be necessary for the responsible JAG officer to fly back to Washington with one or more proposed settlements, secure the approval of the secretary of the Air Force, and then return to the scene prepared to make payment.

The standard for evaluating the success of this mission should not be the niggardliness of the payments made, nor should it be the largess of the Air Force. It should be rather the fair and equitable settlement of claims arising from havoc which the government has unintentionally worked upon the lives of people. If this were the standard of measurement, and if the settlement process were as open as it was fair and expeditious, not only would justice be served by the government having acted responsibly but, in addition, the public image of the administering agency would benefit from that performance.

Epilogue

Disaster is generic. When it happens again, we may be sure that the new incident will vary from the old. A jet passenger plane may break up over the city; a bomber with a small fuel load may glide to the ground rather than invert, taking with it a broad swath of homes, business establishments, and people. A tornado may strike—no new experience to Wichita—or an event may occur which is so unique that it cannot be anticipated.

And when it happens again, there is every likelihood that community responses will be similar to those of January, 1965. Wichitans in municipal and county roles and in private eleemosynary and business institutions have become accustomed to thinking in terms of the possible imminence of disaster. The Disaster Committee continues to function and to review the relative roles of its expanded membership in the event of varying emergencies. They have no illusion, however, that it is possible to categorize possible incidents and establish formulas for automated response. What they seek is the ability to act in a manner which is disciplined and coordinated, yet flexible enough to be adaptive to any event.

Ad hoc groups inevitably will form, their efforts complementing, duplicating, or conflicting with those of official agencies. There will be failures—to anticipate problems which could have been anticipated, to execute plans which have been formulated, to communicate effectively. Personal and group indignation will be engendered, probably with good reason.

If the disaster is occasioned by the crash of a government plane, the new Federal Tort Claims procedures instituted in January, 1967, should expedite immeasurably that restitution which can be made in a nonadversary proceeding. As we have seen, however, the tone characterizing the remedial efforts of the agency which worked harm remains vital. The federal government—especially the Defense Department—has yet to decide, through Congress and through its individual agencies, how callous and tight-fisted a supposedly responsible government can appropriately act toward citizens whom it has harmed.

The bedrock fact remains that if the disaster occurs in a community which, like Wichita, has learned to live with the prospect and to anticipate and plan for it, a city which has built a demonstrated capacity to add improvisation to planning according to the circumstances of the event, that community will respond effectively, minimize the impact, and accelerate recovery.

This capacity is not inbred in communities. The existence of police and fire departments and of civil defense agencies, does not guarantee effective, expeditious, organized *community* response to a disaster. This comes only if time and energy are invested in prior planning. The public and private community leaders having roles to play in the event of disaster, must know one another personally and the roles each plays in time of emergency. When the need arises, they must be able to function virtually without direction. A striking aspect of the Wichita crash was the seeming absence of leadership in the vital hour between 9:30 and 10:30 Saturday morning. The response was not completely spontaneous or extemporized, although, as with all disasters, it did contain those elements. It had been so well discussed in advance that people automatically played the roles they were supposed to; it was this multiplicity of interlocking leadership which obscured the effectiveness of leadership in response to the crash, as did the efficiency of the rank-and-file. It is evidence of the operational effectiveness of the planning which Charles Straub had initiated a decade earlier, and in which he continued to play a key role, that he, knowing there was no function for an airport manager to play at the scene of the crash, proceeded to his office at the airport. A crash response, to be effective, must also be economical; and leaders who had no leadership role to play at the scene of the disaster refrained from confusing organized activity by their presence in the role of spectators.

A final word concerning the victims is appropriate.

In the spring of 1967, two years after the crash, members of two Wichita churches, one Negro, the other predominantly white, heard rumors that crash victims were still in varying kinds of distress and determined to ascertain the facts. Their purpose was twofold: to afford relief where appropriate and possible, and to frame policy recommendations for the handling of such cases in the future. The "Fair-Mark" Committee which undertook this inquiry sought to make contact with 105 people whose names were taken from various lists of those directly or indirectly affected by the disaster. They employed a questionnaire which was filled out by the interviewer in personal contact with the subject.[1]

Of seventy-six contacts, sixty-six responses were usable. Twenty-one per cent of the respondents were involved in litigation. (This means that contact was made with thirteen of the thirty litigants.) Eight per cent of the total number of respondents had not litigated, but expressed the wish that they had consulted an attorney concerning timely action to redress wrongs they thought they had suffered. Twenty-two per cent remembered filling in Air Force forms and 54 per cent thought they had had some contact with the Air Force. Twenty per cent had received Air Force help immediately after the crash. Of the entire group of sixty-six, 79 per cent expressed unhappiness with the way that they had been treated by the Air Force or other agencies involved in responding to the disaster. Twenty-one per cent reported that they were in immediate need of help. It is interesting to note that of all those reporting property damage, only 3 per cent said they were in need of help at the time of interview. Of those suffering personal injury, 45 per cent reported they were in need. This suggests, not unexpectedly, that persons physically or psychically hurt by a crash of this type will have problems which linger longer and which, unless the victim is well off, will be a continuing financial burden. Or it suggests that they will be more cognizant of their problems than are others.

Perhaps the moral of the story is that it does not suffice to attempt to do the "right" thing under such conditions as the KC-135 crash in Wichita. It is crucially necessary, also, to persuade those who have been helped that they have been helped, and that they have received the kind and amount of aid they require from the source responsible for providing it. No crash is going to leave a wake of satisfaction in the community in which it has taken a toll of lives and property. No crash need leave the wake of dissatisfaction and the protracted disruption of lives that has characterized the federal government's response to that which occurred in Wichita, January 16, 1965.

Appendices

Appendix A—The Death Toll

MILITARY PERSONNEL ON AIRCRAFT:

Name:	*Rank:*	*AFSN:*	*Orgn:*	*Hometown:*
Czeslaw Szmuc	Capt	A03005654	902 AREFS	N. Royalton, Ohio
Gary J. Widseth	Capt	A03102539	902 AREFS	Minneapolis, Minn.
Arthur W. Sullivan	2nd Lt	A03139303	902 AREFS	Miami, Fla.
Reginald Went	SSgt	AF13262599	902 AREFS	Baltimore, Md.
Joseph W. Jenkins	SSgt	AF15524866	70th OMS	Middlesboro, Ky.
Daniel E. Kenenski	A1C	AF11396952	70th OMS	Harrisville, R.I.
John L. Davidson	A2C	AF13758031	70th OMS	Philadelphia, Pa.

CIVILIANS:

Name:	*Address:*	*Age:*
Gary L. Martin	2031 N. Piatt	17
Joe T. Martin, Jr.	2031 N. Piatt	25
Clyde Holloway	2037 N. Piatt	44
Tracy Randolph	2037 N. Piatt	5
Dewey Stevens	2037 N. Piatt	66
Claude L. Daniels	2037 N. Piatt	32
Mary Daniels	2037 N. Piatt	56
Julia A. Maloy	2041 N. Piatt	8
Julius R. Maloy	2041 N. Piatt	6
Laverne Warmsley	2041 N. Piatt	25
Emmit Warmsley, Jr.	2041 N. Piatt	12
Emmit Warmsley, Sr.	2041 N. Piatt	37
Ernest E. Pierce, Jr.	2047 N. Piatt	46
Delwood Coles	2047 N. Piatt	34
Albert L. Bolden	2053 N. Piatt	22
Wilma J. Bolden	2053 N. Piatt	24
Leslie I. Bolden	2053 N. Piatt	9 Mo.
Denise M. Jackson	2053 N. Piatt	6
Brenda J. Dunn	2053 N. Piatt	5
Cheryl A. Dale	2059 N. Piatt	2
Alice Dale	2059 N. Piatt	47
James L. Glover	2101 N. Piatt	22

Appendix B

Disaster Committee 7

Wichita Municipal Airport
December 24, 1964

On Thursday, December 24, 1964, a meeting was held which included all the Fire Fighting agencies of the City, including Civil Defense Heavy Rescue and Fire Reserves. Representatives of the County Fire Department were not in attendance, no doubt because of an accident hospitalizing two of their men and destroying a piece of equipment. Those present were:

Keith A. McCarty, Boeing Fire Marshal
Warren Robinson, Captain, Boeing Fire Unit
Robert L. Simpson, Wichita Fire Department
L. D. Carney, Wichita Fire Department
F. J. Kailer, Wichita Fire Department
Tom McGaughey, Wichita Fire Department
Russell O. Dear, Civil Defense
Robert E. Martin, Civil Defense Rescue
Dan E. Anderson, Wichita Fire Reserve
Wm. A. Trotter, Ass't Chief, McConnell AFB
Dale Sedbrook, McConnell AFB
C. Booth, Airport
C. Edward Straub, Airport

Our original chart, dated June 8, 1959, was examined and compared with a suggested revision showing new possible additions to be considered. Although the County was not present it was generally thought that the method being used to signal the fire departments was working satisfactorily and that no changes be made. This was checked with Chief Davis of the County Fire Department later.

The possibility of McConnell being connected with the Fire and Police dispatchers on the present drop was discussed. The City and County have mutual aid agreements, but there is considerable difficulty in the Fire Chiefs of the City and County getting in on the telephone at the Air Base. The Air Force Representative from McConnell who was present at the meeting of the Security people on December 3rd indicated that McConnell was interested in being wired in on this drop from the Control Tower to the Fire and Police Dispatchers. This drop would be in the Command Post at McConnell and would provide the Fire Chiefs with a very desirable communication link between all parties concerned with fire and police activities. The drop would operate differently with McConnell as a participant than it does at present. All of our emergencies are relayed from the Control Tower to the Fire and Police Dispatchers—some thirty calls per year, except for service check calls. The Air Base would use it normally as an advisory source except when called for directly. It is to be remembered that whenever any one phone is picked up at any end, all phones on the line ring. There appeared to be satisfactory communication between Boeing, the City Fire Department and McConnell AFB. It was left to the Fire Chiefs of Boeing, McConnell, and the City-County Chiefs to handle whatever support requests and responses that might come up. It appeared that there were satisfactory arrangements whereby the proper exchange of information would be made to the proper parties if and when Boeing might be called upon. Boeing and McConnell keep each other informed of any of their respective equipment. The County has contact with their Auxiliary Firemen, as has the City Fire Department with their Fire Reserve and the Civil Defense Heavy Rescue. It developed that the Fire Reserve does not have adequate equipment and the City Fire Chief is thinking of possibly using some of the Airport fire equipment. It also developed that there is a lack of communication between the Fire Reserve Equipment, the Heavy Rescue Equipment, and the City Fire Department. Mr. Russell Dear and Dan E. Anderson were going to look into the possibility of some police equipment being available that might be adapted to their communication needs. They should have the City Fire Equipment frequencies. McConnell AFB has two helicopter fire teams that can, if available, be called upon to assist the City and County Departments. The matter of equipment will be left to the Fire Chiefs rather than appear in any summary as is intended here.

Normally at the Airport, the Command Post for the Police and Security will be located at the Administration Building with the Airport Management Office at the center of operations. Should the Fire Chief (City) believe that it is necessary, he may set up his command post Bus adjacent to this point. Communications between the site of the crash and the Command Post will then be located at this point, for both Police and Fire. Fire Reserve Equipment of course will be passed through Police lines but all other persons and equipment should be required to pass through Security before getting on the airport landing area itself. All News Media will get their instructions and transportation from that point. Always in the past the chain of command for the Fire Chiefs passed from the Airport fire equipment, to Cessna's Chief, then to the County Chief, and then to the City Fire Chief. This was based on the time of arrival. There seems no reason to change from this practice. If situation should arise where the scene of the crash would be in the County, or on the Air Base, the passing of responsibility from one chief to another to the proper Fire Authority seems simple enough. Where the crash relates to a military aircraft the matter of information, communication, explosion potential make a picture which is readily understood by the different Fire Chiefs. Rescue operations first if possible, and then withdrawal until military guidance is available through the Base Fire or other source satisfactory to the particular Fire Chief. The Fire Chiefs have already reached an agreement among themselves as to how this should be handled. The Bus operated by the Fire Department is equipped with generator, space for additional radio equipment, and for limited hospital work. It also has refrigeration, etc. This will be something for the medical teams to be familiar with, that is in addition to other similar equipment which would be brought into service by the Red Cross and other Medical Teams.

It was pointed out that there have been several new developments in communication and organization in the Civil Defense, Red Cross, and the local hospitals. There will be a meeting later with National Defense Transportation Association and this will be an opportunity to provide for transportation to supplement the City ambulance service. In a large aircraft carrying approximately 150 people there would be an immediate lack of ambulance type vehicles and it may be necessary to press into service some type of vehicle capable and serviceable for carrying a large number of people to hospitals. All parties to this meeting are asked to contribute anything that has been left out of this summary which might be of importance. . . .

It was also further suggested that as soon as we have the Medical Section and the FAA interviewed and informed as to how they will be alerted and how their activity fits into the picture, that we have a test run of the alert and see just how well the whole plan works. The plan will have to be well checked since there are several hundred people and a number of services involved in the plan. Briefly, the plan breaks down into a normal emergency which takes into action only the City and County Fire Equipment and the City, County, and State Patrol Departments. This involves from seven to ten pieces of Fire apparatus and the Police Authorities. When a Disaster Alert is given this places into motion several hundred people, ambulances, Civil Defense, Fire, Police, Heavy Rescue Services, Red Cross, hospitals, and whatever the Air Force Base is free to send. This is a considerable addition and will require some practice to smooth out communications, location of Morgue, Medical Officials location, etc.

C. Edward Straub
Airport Manager

Appendix C

Wichita Municipal Airport
January 27, 1965
SUBJECT: Fire and Crash Procedure

On January 27, 1965, a meeting was held to review the operation of the Airport Fire & Crash Procedures as applied to the crash of the Jet Tanker in the northeast part of Wichita on Saturday, January 16, 1965. Following are the names of those who attended:

Bill Friesen .... Civil Defense
Capt. Richard Crist .... McAFB—Disaster Control
Dale Sedbrook .... McAFB Fire Chief
A. W. Schara .... McAFB TAC Hospital
Dr. Leonard Hurch .... Director Sedgwick County Hospital
Major George W. Tussing ...... McAFB Director of Operations & Training
Major Charles Prouse .... Wichita Police Department
Pat Kelly .... Red Cross—Disaster Chairman
Harris Burton .... Red Cross—Director of Safety
Ken Thompson .... President—Gold Cross Ambulance
Dr. George L. Thorpe .... St. Joseph—Director of Out Patient Services
C. F. Hybki .... Dept. of Public Health—Educational Services
K. A. McCarty .... Fire Marshal—Boeing
Shelby Smith .... Security Manager—Boeing
R. A. Davis .... Sedgwick County Fire Department
L. E. McCabe .... Sedgwick County Fire Department
Lyle Huitt .... Kansas Highway Patrol
H. E. Starr .... Kansas Highway Patrol
D. E. Dullea .... Secy-Treas. Hospital Council
R. E. Stone .... St. Francis—Ass't Administrator
Dr. D. M. Thompson .... St. Francis—Emergency
A. E. Rickenbrode .... Sheriff's Department
Vern Miller .... Sheriff
Dr. Leon Bauman .... Director of Health Department
E. M. Pond .... Chief, Wichita Police Department
Dr. R. M. Daniels .... Coroner
Dr. Reals .... St. Josephs—Pathologist
Joseph A. Heeb .... St. Josephs—Associate Administrator

Dana Humen	Topeka Police Department
Ray L. McKinney	Topeka Police Department
Cliff Palmer	Topeka Fire Department
Russ Collins	Topeka Fire Department
Bob Simpson	Wichita Fire Department
Tom McGaughey	Wichita Fire Department
C. Edward Straub	Airport Manager
C. Booth	Assistant Airport Manager

From all the contacts that we have made with those who were at the scene and who participated in the disaster, there was a unanimous opinion that the refresher opportunity of going over the procedures and what could be expected at such a situation were much appreciated. The Fire and Police Chiefs felt that having gone over the procedures, the things to be provided, location of morgue, tagging of bodies, activities of the various organizations had been unexpectedly alert and efficient. An example of this was that of Mr. Ken Thompson, President of Gold Cross Ambulance, who was acting as dispatcher and alerter of the hospitals. On the Friday evening preceding the disaster, Mr. Thompson and myself were counting available ambulances. The Medical Association and the other medical men had advised against having semi-trailers to handle mass ambulance cases. They suggested that not more than four and preferably two patients to an ambulance. This required Mr. Thompson to personally contact the mortuaries and alert them to his need. They had responded with 19, which together, with 10 he had between Gold Cross and Metropolitan Ambulance, and 5 which Mr. McReynolds of the Post Office had just that afternoon agreed to offer on any 24 hour basis, made 34 ambulances total as of Friday night. General agreement among the hospital representatives was that Mr. Thompson, acting as dispatcher for disaster ambulance and the source of alert for the hospitals was an improvement from previous practices. Also, we shall have to include Public Health and the County Hospital as part of the alert chart. Actually the Hospital will be included under the activity of the Ambulance Dispatcher.

The discussion disclosed that there is need for a check list for the dispatchers to follow on account of the interruptions and the need to have a list to check and remind him where to pick up his alerting procedure. It is important that such a list make provision for noting and notifying when the emergency is over. The hospitals reported that without exception they were entirely satisfied with the handling of the emergency. Their facilities were over staffed and prepared. The Civil Defense Director had the tags prepared which were used and there were a number of suggestions that developed with regard to tagging. The heat from the charred bodies was sufficient to burn or scorch the paper tags. The military also placed tags as part of their investigation. We understand that they placed 1200 tags. There was some talk of having three copies and that metal pins be available for marking ground locations. The matter of rope was a critical item but it appeared solved by Civil Defense and McConnell Air Force Base. There was a great need for rope standards which evidently was overcome but required many more police than should have been necessary. Once standards were provided and the area roped the curious appeared to obey the restriction very well.

There are several areas in which the notification should be much improved. The hospitals should be notified as to how many casualties are to be handled and any other pertinent information. In a disaster where there would be a greater number of people than in this instance such information would be of great assistance to the hospitals. In this case the hospitals were ready to handle hundreds of casualties. There was a great deal of unnecessary work done that could have been saved and a shorter time for volunteers to have returned to their other duties and jobs.

Indications were, however, that there will now be no necessity for a dry run because this disaster was an all out endeavor. Much of its value will now be to finalize the routines and review the things to be remembered for later situations. All parties were asked to review the chart and select the department under which they would be alerted and give as complete a breakdown with names and services, with the people to be initially alerted clearly indicated. The interest evidenced was gratifying, but we shall have to do all work in advance and submit it to the group for their suggestions. It is advisable to have smaller groups, but there was so much interest that it was difficult to keep those in attendance down. We expected to have only 24, but 36 was the number that were there for information. The Fire and Police Chiefs from Topeka came down for this one reason, and they and McConnell took all of our original procedures for hijacking of airplanes, anonymous phone calls, bomb scare, high explosive fire and crash, as well as our Airport Fire and Crash Procedures.

We shall work up a new chart and submit it to them as a reminder to get in their breakdown, names, services, etc.

C. Edward Straub
Airport Manager

Appendix D

MEETING OF FEBRUARY 18, 1966
SUBJECT: CRASH AND DISASTER PROCEDURES

A noon meeting was held February 18th at the Dobbs House Dining Room. A list of those in attendance is attached. It will be noted that we had almost 100% of key department and administrative heads of the Wichita Sedgwick County Crash and Disaster Procedures. Those not in attendance were contacted shortly after the meeting and acquainted with the important phases of the meeting as they related to their particular department. These minutes should serve as a more permanent reminder. It is noted that the attendance in these meetings has consistently improved and a number of those attending voiced their increasing admiration that so many people who head our communities' public services can find the time to concretely express their personal interest and give witness to the continuing and effective organizing of those services and people in their fields for emergency duty beyond the call of their normal daily commitment. It is also evident that much work and preparation is going on in the various departments, especially the medical specialists, nurses, and hospitals. The organization chart for the Wichita-Sedgwick County area is but a very sketchy abbreviation for the complex and extensive services being made available under the procedures for emergency services. At least one meeting is held each year to re-acquaint the various members with changes in personnel and procedures. No changes in the procedures were made at this meeting. One correction is to be made under the caption of the Medical Society's Air Disaster Committee. This comes under the ambulance dispatcher's notification echelon. Please delete the word "Air" from the Medical Committee caption. There are actually two separate committees that are alerted under this caption, one for air and one for other than air disaster.

The reason for holding the meeting at this time was to make use of a training operation being staffed by the members of the Sixth District of the Nurses Association, as part of a workshop session being conducted by the Disaster Nursing Services Committee of the American Red Cross. Miss Lucille Cook is Vice Chairman of the Red Cross Disaster Committee and Chief of Personal Health Services, Wichita Sedgwick County Health Department. Miss Roberta Thiry is President of the Sixth District of the Nurses Association. The exercise will consist of the setting up of a complete 200 bed emergency mobile hospital. They not only intend to set it up, but they are going to simulate its actual use under emergency conditions. Only those familiar with the complex requirements of such an undertaking can accurately gauge what these people are taking on in the way of a work load. Members of the workshop will be on hand to evaluate their co-workers' effectiveness and efficiency. Medical staff and supporting groups have already been contacted or will be prior to the exercise which will take place in the afternoon of March 16th. Mrs. Julia Jacobus, Chief Disaster Feeding Crew, American Red Cross, left no doubt in any of our minds but that hunger would be effectively dealt with in the coming exercise. Mr. George Wallace, Director of Disaster Services for the American Red Cross, serves as Director of both State and Local Chapters; Harris Burton, Director of Safety Services for the Local Chapter of the American Red Cross, serves also as Assistant Manager of the local chapter; and Tom Irving is Manager of the local Chapter of the Red Cross. Mr. Irving was absent on account of illness. He was represented by Mr. Vernon Clark of the Wichita Civil Defense under Director Bill Friesen. Mr. Clark also serves with Mr. Irving as a member of the Steering Committee of the Nursing Services and the Hospital Exercise. Each of the above persons detailed the nature of the exercise to be performed on March 16th.

The mobile hospital has been assigned by the State Health Services to be used in the State of Kansas and available at all times through the American Red Cross and Civil Defense as required. In order to identify this alert and avoid any confusion as to what is taking place it has presently been determined that the alerting message will be as follows: "Emergency Hospital Exercise 1966—Tornado: Ninth and Edgemoor." Should the location or nature of the disaster be changed, only that after *1966* will be different in the message.

The responsibility for coordination, activation, notification, evaluation as emergency forces are gathered or released, authority beyond the normal operation of the police powers, general overall supervision, and final termination, all fall under the office of our Director of Civil Defense, Mr. Bill Friesen. Mr. Friesen will initiate the alert and will schedule the release of the various phases of our emergency procedures as the exercise progresses. He would like for those who head the various echelons to record the time the message was received and the method by which it was delivered; whatever action was taken (imaginary or otherwise) and when the termination notice was received. Was the message clear? You do not even have to make all the phone calls except to estimate the length of time it took you to reach your people with the alert.

CRASH AND DISASTER PROCEDURES ALERTING COMMUNITY FACILITIES FOR THE PROTECTION AND SAVING OF LIVES AND PROPERTY IN THE WICHITA-SEDGWICK COUNTY AREA

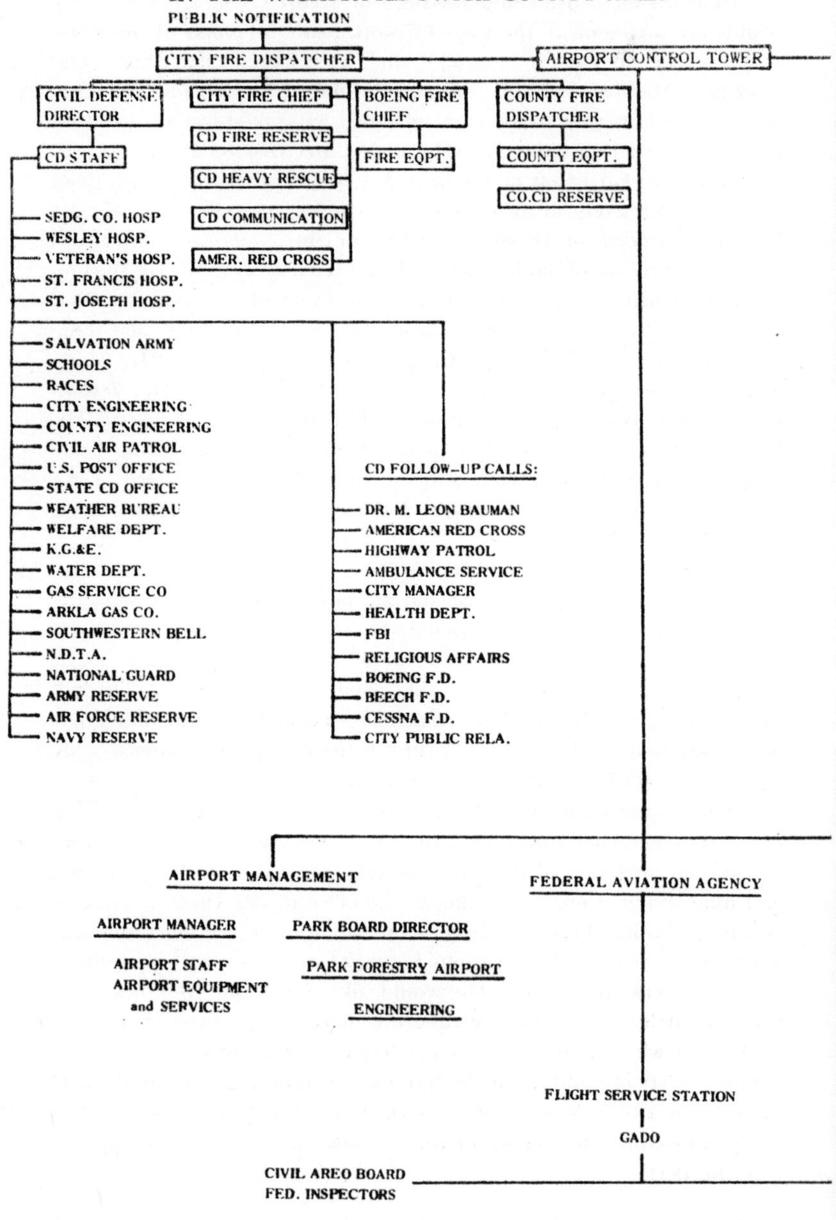

CRASH AND DISASTER PROCEDURES ALERTING COMMUNITY FACILITIES FOR THE PROTECTION AND SAVING OF LIVES AND PROPERTY IN THE WICHITA-SEDGWICK COUNTY AREA

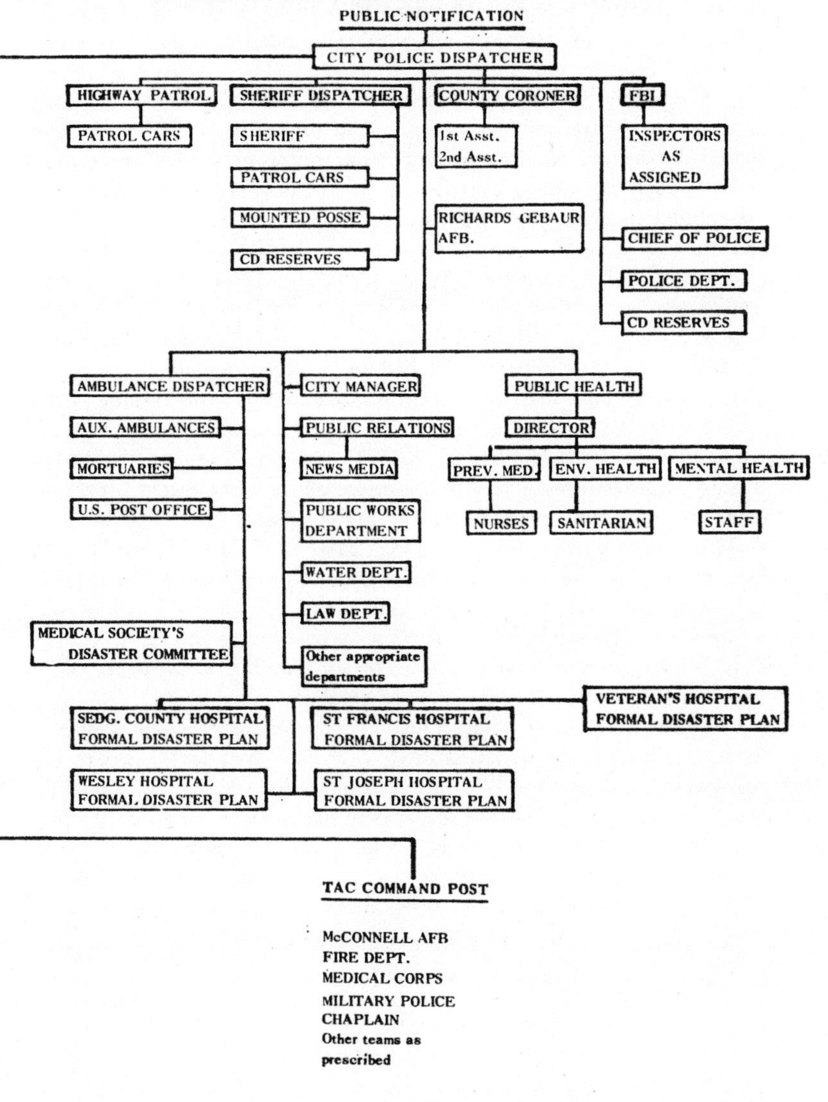

U.S. POST OFFICE
POSTAL INSPECTORS

Mr. Friesen made clear that the response required to this alert is entirely up to the head of the agency alerted and to the various task forces within his echelon who might wish to be alerted or to actually participate. Should there be any doubts or questions, please call Mr. Friesen.

A separate and simple procedure has been developed over the years at the Municipal Airport to make provision for the Press and Radio during the conduct of emergency procedures. This procedure has also been expanding somewhat so that certain of the provisions may be applied in areas other than at the Airport. Due to the change in personnel and closer cooperation between Press, Radio, and the Fire and Police, it has been thought beneficial to have a meeting perhaps once a year or as it appears advisable. A meeting was held with these people on February 17th in order to permit the Police, Fire, Air Force, Coroner, State Highway, and the Federal Aviation Agency to exchange views, correct misunderstandings, and to announce the coming alert. There were 28 in attendance. This meeting also provides an opportunity for the Press, Radio, and TV to communicate their problems during coverage of an emergency to those officials who might otherwise come to present an uncompromising and uncooperative force in their daily task of supplying the public with facts on the passing world. We feel certain that knowing the other workman's problem can be a great help in getting our own job done, and many times actually being able to assist a fellow workman at the same time. During the meeting they were briefed on the details of the exercise simulated emergency alert and they will be ready to cover the operation.

We mention this separate meeting because these members of the Press and Radio will be acquainted with their part in the severe occurrences that will take place in our community and thereby they can better present to the public the efforts made under your emergency procedures and more intelligently report on the efforts being made by your organizations to serve the people under emergency conditions. You will be able to recognize these press and radio people by their Armbands or auto cards which in large letters reads "NEWS."

ATTENDING MEETING OF FEBRUARY 18, 1966

1. Roberta D. Thiry .... Ass't Director, Wesley School of Nursing, Chairman ARC Nursing Services
2. M/Sgt R. Gold .... 381 SMW SAC Disaster Control
3. S/Sgt Richard O. Bunch .... McAFB Disaster Control
4. M/Sgt F. C. Scroggins .... 835th TAC Hospital McAFB
5. Keith A. McCarty .... Boeing Fire Marshal

6. Wm. A. Trotter .... McAFB—Ass't Chief
7. Homer E. Hall .... Deputy Chief, Wichita Fire Department
8. Bob Simpson ...... Deputy Chief, Wichita Fire Department
9. R. A. Davis .... Sedgwick Co. Fire Department
10. L. E. McCabe .... Sedgwick Co. Fire Department
11. Tom McGaughey .... Wichita Fire Department
12. Byron L. Dozer .... Chief Fire Dispatcher, Wichita Fire Department
13. R. F. Linehan .... Ass't Chief, Wichita Tower, FAA
14. Warren P. Hurst .... Chief, Flight Service Station Wichita, FAA
15. Ramon L. Wert, Capt. .... Salvation Army, Wichita
16. Lucile Cook, RN .... Chief Nursing Services, PH Dept. RC, Chairman Disaster
17. Julia A. Jacobus .... Disaster Feeding Crew, ARC
18. George Wallace .... ARC
19. Harris Burton .... ARC
20. Vernon W. Clark .... Civil Defense
21. C. F. Hybki .... County Health Department
22. D. E. Dullea .... St. Francis Hospital
23. R. E. Stone .... St. Francis Hospital
24. Bill Friesen .... Civil Defense
25. Joe Heeb .... St. Joseph Hospital
26. Dr. George L. Thorpe .... St. Joseph Hospital
27. Dr. Lewis Marshall .... St. Joseph Hospital
28. Wm. F. Schaffer .... St. Joseph Hospital
29. James H. Foster .... Wichita Police Department
30. Charles Prowse .... Wichita Police Department
31. Joe Klepper .... Wichita Police Department
32. Claud Nichols .... Wichita Police Department
33. Ken Thompson .... Gold Cross Ambulance
34. Dwight Allen .... Medical Society
35. R. L. Davis .... Chief of Security, Wesley Medical Center
36. K. M. Duckworth .... Wichita Police Department
37. L. R. Hadsall .... Kansas Highway Patrol, Valley Center
38. Guy Livengood .... Kansas Highway Patrol, Valley Center
39. Dr. Bob Tinker .... Sedgwick County Medical Society
40. Dr. Leonard Hirsch .... Sedgwick County Hospital Supt.
41. Larry Barrett .... Trans World Airlines
42. Dave Cotten .... PIO, City of Wichita
43. C. Booth .... Assistant Airport Manager
44. C. Edward Straub .... Airport Manager

Appendix E

SUBJECT: PARK BOARD FIRE & CRASH PHONE

A meeting was held Tuesday, April 5, 1966, for the purpose of reviewing and re-establishing procedures for the use of the Crash and Disaster phone. This phone serves as the basis of alerting the facilities of our Wichita-Sedgwick County Crash & Disaster Procedures, which has evolved from our Airport Fire & Crash Procedures. The agencies that compose the elements of this procedure are more specifically set forth in the Crash and Disaster Procedures chart, dated February 18, 1966, attached herewith.

Those attending this meeting were:

Major Ange Delbon, Disaster Control Representative from McAFB

Captain Joseph Dupont, Jr., Disaster Control Representative from McAFB

Mr. Byron Dozer, Chief Dispatcher for the Wichita Fire Department

Captain Kenneth Duckworth, Chief Dispatcher for the Wichita Police Department

Mr. Richard F. Linehan, Ass't Chief of the Wichita Control Tower

C. Edward Straub, Airport Manager, Board of Park Commissioners

The McConnell Air Force Base is now installing a telephone drop on the Crash and Disaster Phone System. It is located in the Tactical Command Post with an auxiliary drop connected to the Disaster Control Console adjacent thereto. TAC Command Post is manned at all times. The AFB Disaster Control position is staffed at irregular intervals but may be activated almost immediately upon receipt by TAC of certain qualifying information. Pre-arranged assignments may be instantly placed into action.

The following Procedures are agreed upon; effective date May 1, 1966, 07:00 CT

STANDARD OPERATING PROCEDURES RELATING TO THE USE OF THE CRASH AND DISASTER PHONE

A. All rings to stations other than the Control Tower indicate a DISASTER CONFERENCE, MUNICIPAL AIRPORT EMERGENCY, OF A TEST CALL.

B. The FIRE DISPATCHER will answer all rings from the Control Tower. All other stations on the line will MONITOR ONLY. Depending upon the nature of the call the Fire Dispatcher will make the decision as to whether there will be a poll of the conference line to determine that all parties are present on the conference line. The Fire Dispatcher will then advise the reason for the call. The information to be acted upon will then be stated by the authority initiating the conference. *UNLESS CALLED BY THE FIRE DISPATCHER ALL STATIONS ON THE LINE WILL MONITOR ONLY.*

C. Except for multiple disaster conferences, once the Disaster Conference has been made, the initiation of further communications over the Disaster Phone should be unnecessary. The system is not designed for convenience, information, or the state of emergency progress. It is ALERTIVE ONLY to those agency heads set forth in the Procedures. *ALL CALLS* are *URGENT*. Be alert in receiving and precise in transmitting.

The following may be of use in understanding the operation of the Phone Line:

PHYSICAL OPERATION OF THE PHONE SYSTEM

A. When the Control Tower Operator picks up his crash phone all phones ring simultaneously. All Stations are on a conference line.

B. When a station other than the Control Tower picks up its phone ONLY the Control Tower is signaled. The initiating station and the Control Tower are the only parties on the line.

C. For a DISASTER CONFERENCE to take place when initiated by a station other than the Control Tower:—Pick up the Crash Phone and when the Control Tower acknowledges, identify the Station calling and request a DISASTER CONFERENCE. The request delivered and received both the Station and the Control Tower hang up their instruments.
The Control Tower Operator will pause three seconds and will again pick up the DISASTER PHONE to initiate the conference line.

BRIEF HISTORY

Originally the Crash Phone was the means of communication for emergency purposes between the Airport Management and the Control Tower. The Termination points were changed to place emergency phones in the ready room of Aircraftco Service, and the Dispatcher's Office of the Wichita Fire Department. Separate written procedures supplemented this arrangement so that other emergency services were alerted. The Office of the Police Dispatcher of the Wichita Police Department was added in order to control automotive traffic. The other emergency service arrangements were expanded to take in the State Highway Patrol, the Sheriff's Office, and the Civilian Defense Emergency Services. The Procedures were then expanded to serve the Community and those additional facilities set forth on the Crash and Disaster Procedures were formulated and rehearsed just prior to the Jet Tanker Crash. The addition now of the McConnell AFB will greatly increase the effectiveness and the scope of response possible relating to a disaster in this vicinity. It is expected that further agreements of a mutual assistance nature will be arranged in the future between those facilities present on the Procedure Chart. Those now present on the Crash and Disaster Phone are:

1. Wichita Municipal Airport Control Tower
2. Aircraftco Services, Inc., Wichita Municipal Airport
3. Wichita Fire Department Dispatcher
4. Wichita Police Department Dispatcher
5. McConnell AFB, TAC Command Post & Disaster Control Officer

Once this key group is placed into action the alarm spreads through prearranged telephone and radio networks to include the facilities which appear in the procedures. All these groups are prepared, trained, and organized to cooperatively or independently support the efforts of constituted authority in effectuating recovery from and control over emergencies beyond the normal capabilities of the individual participating facilities. The Civil Defense Director serves to introduce and train new services and facilities as they appear in our community. The depth of the response is left to the discretion and judgment of the various department heads in the pyramid. Each unit develops and keeps current its own emergency procedures. Once each year the Administrative Heads on the Procedures assemble to discuss and to become personally acquainted with one another and with the supportive procedures involved. A separate meeting is held also with members of the Press and Radio to keep contact with them in the recognition of the mutuality of the services operating in emergency and the responsibilities which constituted authority has and the necessity for cooperative efforts on the part of the News Media in order that all parties can do their work. The members of the News Media have been issued Arm Bands with reflective lettering saying "NEWS" which identifies them on the airport. Statements have been signed by the newsmen recognizing the dangers inherent in entering emergency areas. It is hoped that some day it will be required that newsmen be required by ordinance to recognize certain authority and protocol when entering emergency areas. Members of the News Media have been warned and advised that any pictures of military aircraft or personnel must be cleared by the Air Force Public Information Officer before the photographer leaves the scene. This briefing was done by members of the McConnell AFB Disaster Control who were present at a called meeting for the News and Police. The Federal Aviation Agency authorities are interested in any pictures of civil aircraft taken by photographers. Except as directed by the appropriate authorities all wreckage should remain in place. There are Federal penalties for violations of this requirement. This is repeated here for the benefit of those concerned who may read copies of the Memorandum.

The line of authority for fire is passed from the first Fire Chief on the scene to the Fire Chief in whose jurisdiction the disaster occurs; the same for police authority. With respect to off-base emergencies involving military aircraft, the authority over the aircraft and everything pertaining to such aircraft is understood by the civil authorities. Full cooperation will be given by all parties. The recognition over such aircraft and contents in no way supercedes or abrogates the responsibilities of the Civil authorities in the conduct of the emergency or the measures used by Civil Fire and police authorities in the protection of lives, property, and of maintenance of civil order. All authorities are asked to identify themselves and make their presence known at the location of the emergency command posts at the scene of the disaster.

This points up the advantage of regular meetings between the essential agency heads during the year and for the constant review of these procedures by changing of personnel. Fortunately we have had a tremendous sense of responsibility on the part of administrative heads and individuals in reviews, updating of procedures, and drills. During March a drill was made by the Red Cross which included a simulated emergency in which the Crash and Disaster Procedures were alerted for a tornado at a specific location, and a 200-bed Mobile Hospital with complete services was manned. Participation was unusually complete and included actual operating room activities. Actual disaster conditions were experienced during the recovery operations resulting from the crash of the Jet Tanker. The response was such that all participating in the Procedures felt that the time spent in previous years was well repaid. The basic procedures have been in effect for more than a decade with but very little change or additional administrative load. There are a number of ways in which the system can be improved and it appears that such changes will become a gradual and normal corporate growth.

Notes

Introduction

1. George W. Baker and Dwight W. Chapman, eds., *Man and Society in Disaster* (New York: Basic Books, Inc., 1962), p. 38. Clark's italics.

Chapter I

1. "Stratofortress," *Flight,* Vol. LXII, Part II (1952), 702-4.
2. See "Turbojet Transports by Boeing," *The Aeroplane* (January 27, 1956), pp. 122-6.
3. "The Boeing Company Press Release S-3635 [S-3290 updated]" (January 29, 1966).
4. *Op. cit.*
5. "SAC Press Service 4304RBR-30" (June, 1967).
6. The Boeing Company, *op. cit.* "The actual SAC tanker force is not that large, as some of the planes have been converted to other uses by the Air Force. In addition to the 732 KC-135A's, Boeing built another 88 similar aircraft for other Air Force uses such as flying command posts, pure transports, electronic reconnaisance and photo mapping."
7. *Report of Collateral Investigation Board, KC-135A 54-1442, 16 January, 1965* (Wichita, Kansas), I,29: Testimony of Technical Sergeant William T. Daley, 70th Organizational Maintenance Squadron, Clinton-Sherman AFB, Oklahoma.
8. "SAC Operations Order 83-65 (Lucky Number)," September 11, 1964, *Air Force Report,* Vol. II, Appendix B.
9. Air Force Report, II,7: Testimony of Chief Master Sergeant R. H. Grant, noncommissioned officer in charge, Tanker Flight Line Section, 70th Organizational Maintenance Squadron, Clinton-Sherman AFB, Oklahoma.
10. *Ibid.:* Grant, p. 17.
11. *Iibid.,* pp. 84-87: Testimony of Captain Sidney S. Buswell, tanker scheduler, 70th Bomb Wing.
12. *Ibid.:* Buswell, p. 94.
13. *Ibid.,* p. 74.
14. *Ibid.,* p. 86.
15. *Ibid.,* p. 120.
16. *Ibid.,* pp. 81, 119-20, 135, 186.
17. *Ibid.,* p. 121.
18. *Ibid.,* Exhibits V and P.
19. *Ibid.,* I, 133A-134.
20. *Ibid.,* pp. 184, 179-80.
21. *Ibid.,* pp. 186, 187.
22. *Ibid.,* p. 187.
23. *Ibid.,* II, Exhibit W6.
24. *Wichita Beacon,* January 16, 1965, p. 1.
25. *Wichita Eagle,* January 18, 1965, p. 1. One finds references listing conflicting totals of twenty-nine and of thirty dead. The apparent discrepancy arises from the problem of whether or not to include among the dead the unborn fetus of a pregnant victim.
26. See *Air Force Report,* Vol. II, Exhibit X. For estimate of amount of aircraft debris and lack of ejection mechanism, see *Department of Defense Appropriations* for 1967, Part 6, p. 39ff: Committee on Appropriations, Subcommittee on Department of Defense, which reports on the crash of a KC-135 in Spain during refueling operations with an atomic bomb-laden B-52 on January 17, 1966.
27. *Contrails,* January 22, 1965. ("The *Contrails* is an unofficial newspaper published weekly by Rand Company in the interests of personnel at McConnell Air Force Base.")
28. *Ibid.*
29. *Beacon,* "Crash Investigation started in Minutes," January 19, 1965, p. 1.
30. *Wichita Eagle and Beacon,* Sunday, October 3, 1965, p. 9A. The headline of another story in this edition reads "Mechanical Difficulty Crash Cause."

Chapter V

1. Robert A. Goldwin, ed. *A Nation of States* (Chicago: Rand McNally & Co., 1963), pp. 3, 4.
2. American Telephone and Telegraph *Annual Report,* 1965, p. 10.

Chapter VI

1. Jack Pease, "Thin Line Divided Fate at Crash," *Eagle,* January 17, 1965, p. 3A.
2. *Beacon,* January 16, 1965, p. 3A; and *Eagle and Beacon,* January 2, 1966, p. 17A.
3. *Eagle,* January 17, 1966, p. 5A.
4. The Institute of Logopedics, an affiliate of Wichita State University, is located close to the impact point of the crash.
5. *Eagle,* January 17, 1966, p. 5A.

Chapter VII

1. *Beacon,* July 8, 1967, pp. 1, 3A. This is the fourth in a series of articles on "The Negro in Wichita," which began on July 5 and concluded July 15, 1967. Featured on the front page and accompanied by collateral stories, the series constitutes a straightforward documentation of the segregation of Negroes in Wichita and an indictment of community leaders in general for their casual disregard.
2. *Beacon,* July 7, 1967, p. 1.
3. See John Dundas and Everett Morrow, *A Profile of Wichita,* The Community Planning Council Publication No. 72 (December, 1965); Donald O. Cowgill and F. Samuel Ostertag, Jr., *The People of Wichita* (University of Wichita Center for Urban Studies [January 1962]); and Warren M. Banner, *A Review of the Economic and Cultural Problems of Wichita, Kansas* (National Urban League, New York, [January-February 1965]).
4. Cowgill and Ostertag, *op. cit.*
5. That is, highest incidence in terms of absolute number. It is not to suggest that each of the housing tracts is completely Negro, and, as a matter of fact, Tract No. 7 is the least solidly Negro of the three. Tract No. 6 is 96.2 per cent Negro, No. 8 is 78.7 per cent, and No. 7 is 57.9 per cent. These are 1960 census figures, however, and Tract No. 7 had undoubtedly become more concentratedly Negro in the five years between the census and the crash.
6. The Air Force says, "Although the possibility exists that the pilot nosed the aircraft down to avoid hitting a housing area, the investigation could not establish whether he did or did not take such action." From "KC-135 Accident, Wichita, Kansas, January 16, 1965," Air Force release provided to the author by Congressman Garner E. Shriver, November, 1965.
7. *Beacon,* July 14, 1967, pp. 1, 6A.

Chapter VIII

1. Senator A. S. Mike Monroney of Oklahoma in support of 1961 bill to raise the $5,000 limit for administrative settlement of military claims arising out of the crash of a U.S. Air Force F100-D jet in Midwest City, Oklahoma, August 25, 1961. *Senate Report No. 1085,* 87th Cong., 1st Sess., September 20, 1961, p. 3.
2. The United States Court of Claims was established in 1855, 10 Stat. 612, but for many years its decisions on claims were subject to review and approval by the Secretary of the Treasury. See *Gordon* v. *United States,* 117 U.S. 697 (1868). Further, only claims founded on the Constitution, an Act of Congress, regulations of executive departments, contracts with the government, etc., could be prosecuted there. Until 1946 a citizen enjoyed no right to sue the government for tortious wrongs in the U.S. courts.
3. Title 10 U.S. Code Annotated, Sec. 2733 (a).
4. *Ibid.,* Secs. 2733 (b), (d), (g), and (e).

5. 75 Stat. 488; 10 U.S. Code Annotated, Sec. 2736.
6. H.R. Report No. 104, 89th Cong., 1st Sess., February 24, 1965. P.L. 89-65. The earlier special enactments were P.L. 87-393 covering the Midwest City crash, and P.L. 86-476 which suspended the $5,000 limitation for the Little Rock incident.
7. Kansas Statutes Annotated, Sec. 60-1903, 1904. Effective January 1, 1967, the wrongful death limit was raised to $35,000.
8. H.R. Report No. 104, *op. cit.*, pp. 2-3.
9. *Contrails,* January 22, 1965, p. 6. See note I-27.
10. Letter and Report, April 20, 1967, from Chief of Congressional Inquiry Division, Office of the Secretary, Department of the Air Force.
11. Major (now Lieutenant Colonel) William Cordingly of the McConnell JAG office, quoted in the *Eagle,* September 29, 1965, p. 5A.
12. Guy L. Goodwin, assistant U.S. attorney, letter to author, July 27, 1967. This unsolicited letter—the only contact the author has had with attorneys involved in the KC-135 cases in which pending litigation was discussed—was the indirect result of the author's visit the week of July 17, 1967, with the JAG office, McConnell Air Force Base. A copy of an early draft of this chapter was provided to a JAG officer, who had occasion to read portions of it to the assistant U.S. attorney, resulting in his July 27 letter. As late as July 29, the author was informed of a memorandum which had been prepared by JAG relative to claims processing as depicted in this chapter and was to be made available after clearance with the base commander. By telephone on August 2, 1967, Lt. Col. William Cordingly of the JAG office informed the author he had no obligation or inclination to clear the memorandum and forward it. This action, which conveys an impression of indifference to public opinion, is consistent with treatment received from this office by other groups and individuals making legitimate inquiries.
13. Goodwin, *op. cit.* The emphasis is Mr. Goodwin's.
14. "USAF 'Lack of Response' Brought Crash Suits," p. 5A.
15. *Eagle,* August 5, 1965, pp. 1, 3A.
16. *Eagle,* February 22, 1966, p. 14A.
17. *Beacon,* October 2, 1965, p. 1.
18. *Beacon,* February 27, 1967, p. 12B.
19. *Beacon,* March 28, 1967, p. 12B.
20. *Eagle,* March 29, 1967, p. 3B.
21. Goodwin, *op. cit.* Emphasis is Mr. Goodwin's.
22. *Eagle,* May 27, 1967, p. 1.
23. H.R. Report No. 1532, 89th Cong., 2nd Sess., May 16, 1966, p. 6.
24. "USAF Aircraft Crash, Midwest City, Oklahoma," Report for Congress, August 25, 1961. Carbon of a typescript provided by Senator A. S. Mike Monroney (Oklahoma). This settlement figure is based upon the five cases reported to Congress. The report states that twenty-six other cases were administratively settled within the limits of Air Force's standard discretion under Title 10 U.S. Code Sec. 2733, and parents of two children who lost their lives filed suits under the Federal Tort Claims Act.
25. "USAF Aircraft Crash, Little Rock, Arkansas," Report for Congress, March 31, 1960.
26. Col. William R. Arnold, USAF Chief of Claims Division, Office of the Judge Advocate General, Washington, D.C., in a letter to the author, July 28, 1967. "A case-by-case search of litigation and claim files would be required to provide the requested information."
27. Committee on Armed Services, United States Senate, 87th Con., 1st Sess., Hearing, *Nomination of F. J. Larsen and Miscellaneous Bills,* August 10, 1961, pp. 30-31. While the Air Force deserves credit for introducing such legislation, it is significant that it received such casual committee treatment. Congress appears relatively unconcerned about the

procedures for handling citizen claims against the government, even when it acts upon the matter.

28. H.R. Report No. 791, 87th Cong., 1st Sess., July 24, 1961.
29. H.R. Report No. 1174, 87th Cong., 1st Sess., September 12, 1961.
30. August 5, 1965, p. 1, 3A.
31. February 26, 1966, p. 1C.
32. Dusky E. Broadus, Deputy Clerk, United States District Court, District of Kansas, Wichita, Kansas, letter to the author, July 24, 1967.
33. Goodwin, *op. cit.* Emphasis is Mr. Goodwin's.
34. In a lengthy communication of May 8, 1967, to Representative Garner E. Shriver, who had made inquiry of the Air Force concerning aspects of settlement of constituents' claims under P.L. 89-65 which he sponsored, Colonel Dwight W. Covell of the Congressional Inquiry Division, Office of the Secretary of the Air Force, drew the congressman's attention to the Air Force position that a claimant must choose between the options of administrative settlement in accordance with the Military Claims Act or litigation under the Federal Tort Claims Act. He may not pursue both simultaneously, accepting the disposition which comes through first. This does not preclude withdrawing a court suit and then, within the two-year time period allowed, seeking administrative settlement.

    In making his point, Colonel Covell informed Shriver that the Air Force regards statements to the contrary, contained in a U.S. District Court decision coming from Pennsylvania, as *dicta*—that is, not relevant to the decision of the case on its merits and not binding. *Arkwright Mut. Ins. Co.* v. *Bargain City, U.S.A., Inc.,* 251 F. Supp. 221, U.S. Dist. Ct., E.D. Pa. (1966), which is cited, involves the crash of a U.S. Navy FJ-3 jet aircraft into Bargain City Store No. 10, Horsham, Montgomery County, Pennsylvania, August 27, 1961. The plane, on a noncombat mission, was flown by a naval aviator. Eight months after the crash, on April 23, 1962, the Under Secretary of the Navy communicated to the director of the Bureau of the Budget a recommendation that he report to Congress $156,000 loss of profit and $72,404.34 damage to store fixtures, or $228,404.34 in all, as appropriate settlement. Thirteen months after this recommendation, and approaching two years after the crash, Congress enacted the Supplemental Appropriations Act of May 17, 1963 authorizing payment, and the funds were paid out on June 8, 1963. Since Bargain City had filed a petition in bankruptcy in the U.S. District Court, Eastern District, Pennsylvania, on October 19, 1962, the funds were paid into court.
35. A year and a day after the Wichita crash, a B-52 and KC-135 collided six miles above Palomares, Spain. Four H-bombs were eventually recovered, and this process kept the crash in the headlines for weeks. The 800,000 tons of debris resulting from the crash and the three H-bombs which landed on terrain caused no deaths but considerable damage. The processing of claims appears to have been expeditious and the settlements liberal. However, the claimants seem to be no happier with the result than are those in Wichita. See Flora Lewis, *One of Our H-Bombs is Missing* (New York: McGraw-Hill, 1967).
36. P.L. 89-506, July 18, 1966, 80 Stat. 306.
37. *Improvement of Procedures in Claims Settlement and Government Litigation,* April 6, 1966, H.R., Committee on the Judiciary, Subcommittee No. 2.
38. *Ibid.,* p. 15.
39. *Ibid.,* p. 13. If this language appears to conflict with the data on Federal Tort Claims Act settlements offered earlier from the same source, the reader should keep in mind that here Mr.

Douglas speaks of the "average settlement" — perhaps using the word in a loose sense to suggest "usual" or "modal" — whereas earlier the author took an average of all settlements from the absolute figures given by Douglas.

Epilogue

1. Fairmount Community Church (United Church of Christ), and St. Mark Methodist Church — hence "Fair-Mark."

Index

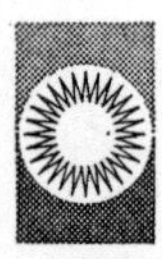

This book was designed by Fritz Reiber. The text was set in 10 pt. Linotype Baskerville leaded 2 pts., headings in 24 pt. Ludlow Bodoni Modern Italics. It was printed on Perkins and Squier RR 60# Standard White by the University of Kansas Printing Service. The cover material is Interlaken Arco Pyroxylin Linen, bound by the State Printer.